How Not To Live Your Life

A comedy novel and self-help parody

Rich Nash

First published in paperback in 2024 by Rich Nash

Copyright © Rich Nash 2024

The right of Rich Nash to be identified as the Author of the Work has been asserted by him in accordance with the Copyright, Designs and Patents Act 1988.

All rights reserved. No part of this publication may be reproduced, stored in a retrieval system, or transmitted in any form or by any means without the prior written permission of the publisher, nor otherwise be circulated in any form of binding or cover other than that in which it is published and without a similar condition being imposed on the subsequent purchaser.

All characters in this publication are fictitious and any resemblance to real persons, living or dead, is purely coincidental.

Artwork by 100 covers.

The book reflects the language, standards, and attitudes of Cuthbert Huntsman, a gratuitously offensive and misguided individual.

An insensitivity reader was employed to ensure that everything is as triggering as possible. If you are affected by any of the issues raised, there is no helpline - just pull yourself together.

Do not under any circumstances follow Cuthbert's advice, unless under the direct supervision of a psychiatrist and an ambulance crew. There is a reason he is an unemployed life coach.

www.cuthberthuntsman.com

Contents

1. RULE 1 - Face Your Fears And Run — 1
2. RULE 2 - Set Yourself Goals And Miss Them — 3
3. RULE 3 - Violence Is Golden — 10
4. RULE 4 - Life Is Like A Box Of Frogs — 22
5. RULE 5 - Gravity Is A Force To Be Reckoned With — 35
6. RULE 6 - Eternity Goes On A Bit — 51
7. RULE 7 - Time Travel Broadens The Mind — 73
8. RULE 8 - Wait Until You're Dead To Get Found Out — 81
9. RULE 9 - Love Is Blind Drunk — 97
10. RULE 10 - Work Hard, Die Hard — 117
11. RULE 11 - The Law Has Long Arms And Hairy Legs — 134
12. RULE 12 - Spiritualism Is Best Kept In Bottles — 165
13. RULE 13 - Revenge Is A Dish Best Served By A Voodoo Priestess — 173
14. RULE 14 - Reality Is Overrated — 189

15.	RULE 15 - What Goes Around Comes Around, But Some People Duck	198
16.	RULE 16 - Cancel Gen Z	232
17.	CONCLUSION - How Not To Live Your Life	239
Review		243
Also By Rich Nash		244
About the Author		245
Follow Cuthbert		247
Free Book		249
Film Adaptations & Options		250

RULE 1 - FACE YOUR FEARS AND RUN

As an unemployed life coach, people often ask me, "Why the hell should I take advice from a homeless, bankrupt, alcoholic junkie with eight failed marriages, seventeen restraining orders and a kidnap conviction for holding his social worker hostage in a wheelie bin?"

This book is my answer: a comprehensive guide for anyone wishing to know how not to live their life. It chronicles my encounters with blurred visionaries and misguided muppets and draws step-by-step conclusions about their catastrophic errors. The Brothers Grimm and Hans Christian Andersen may have collected folk tales from illiterate peasants, but I have harvested textbook cockups from inebriated numpties and assorted weirdoes across the world and distilled their essence into pathetic parables and ridiculous rules. Together, they provide a foolproof guide for anyone wishing to know what not to do.

Before we begin, let's try one of my least popular life coaching techniques - negative visualisation:

Tense up, grit your teeth, and try to ignore your breathing. Remember, it's only air. Think of your happiest memory; then say goodbye to it. Walk up to a mirror and hug your reflection. Hard, isn't it? Blow a love bubble around your family. Prick it and watch them get covered in wet soap. Consider the gibbon. Contemplate its tree-swinging skills, poor hygiene, and dodgy table manners. Then forget it again. Who the hell needs gibbons? Beware Confusion, the cross-eyed monster. Remember, failure's all part of life's rich bicycle, wheels of misfortune turning on cogs of nonsense, moving along The Great Chain of Doubt. Face your fears and run. Set yourself goals and boot the ball as wide as the corner flag. Remember, every silver lining has a cloud. If God hands out lemons, make bitter lemon. Feeling better?

I'm Cuthbert Huntsman (I know, my parents hated me) and these are my rules.

RULE 2 - SET YOURSELF GOALS AND MISS THEM

Sport is a pantomime, with its heroes, villains, and clowns. A last-minute winner can make you a legend, but an own goal, a missed penalty or a defensive howler can consign you to the circus of history. Children may be taught that it's the taking part that matters, but I've long known that not taking part matters more. That doesn't mean I'm not fascinated by failure, particularly failure of the heroic kind. After all, knowing that you are inept and persisting regardless is what makes Britain what it is: a mess.

One Saturday at the grim end of February, I decided to investigate this phenomenon at a ninth-tier football match on the outskirts of an unpopular West Midlands town. The ground was sandwiched between a prison and a donkey sanctuary, and entrance was one-pound-fifty. I joined the other two spectators in a stand the size of a bus stop. The teams stumbled out to an elderly disco ditty farted out on a broken speaker. One linesman was a child, the other was in his seventies, and the ref walked with a limp. The pitch was doubly askew, sloping from goal to goal and from touchline to touchline, and there was a single advertising hoarding for haemorrhoid cream.

South West Birmingham Athletic played in blue and were sponsored by a beautician. North East Ladywood Academicals played in red and were sponsored by a crematorium. Athletic liked passing it out from the back, but always lost possession before the third touch. Academicals attempted route-one football, but always lobbed their own striker. Neither side could defend, shunning both zonal marking and man-marking in favour of menacing stares and violence. Short corners went to the opposition, long corners went out of play and set pieces either hit the wall or the horizon.

There wasn't a lot to see on the pitch, so I watched the other spectators instead. They were a pair of amateur footballers' wives, and no one could accuse them of being underdressed.

A small blonde lady with dappled spray-tan said, "Ace being an AWAG, irrenit, Jen?"

"Bostin, Shel," replied a taller brunette, who dripped junk jewellery, carried a cavernous handbag, and sported an unwieldy pair of sunglasses on her pointy nose.

"Double page spread in The Tamworth Tatler," Shel said.

"And free cider at Nuneaton's second most popular nightspot," Jen said.

A blundering tackle sent a heavy-bellied midfielder crashing into a crater. The ref blew his whistle and limped over. There were no physios, so the player's manager, who looked like an old school bank robber, shouted, "Pull yourself together yer big girl's blouse!" by way of treatment.

Jen and Shel started talking again. I liked them both, though not necessarily in the trouser department. They certainly seemed more entertaining than the match.

"Bostin handbag, Jen."

"Ta, Shel."

"I never knew you spelt *Gucci* with three *c's*."

"It's a genuine fake. Gary bought it off a Thai transsexual at a Patpong ping-pong show."

"It's dead roomy, Jen."

"It's gotta be, Shel. How else am I going to carry Tinkerbell around?"

"Yer pit bull?"

"He's a lovely dog." Jen opened her handbag, revealing a snarling, shark-jawed beast with a skull the size of a cannon ball.

"Yer dog's a bloke?"

"Course, Shel."

"And you call him Tinkerbell?"

"I've always liked Disney."

We all watched the match for a bit. What it lacked in quality, it made up for in incident. A defender nutmegged his own goalkeeper, a striker headed the post with his skull, a midfielder backheeled into his own net, two opposing players missed a drop ball and kicked the ref in both sets of ribs, a goal kick banana-ed backwards for a corner and a winger groined himself on the corner flag. It could have been the final of the Incompetence World Cup. Eventually, my fellow spectators' attention was drawn to a miserable footballer adjusting his shin pad.

"Oh dear, Shel. Your Steve's looking as cheery as a freshly buggered bum hole."

"We had a bit of a tiff, Jen."

"He's never being stingy about your spending again?"

"Too right he is, Jen. Steve just doesn't realise how much it costs to be beautiful."

"What are you gonna get seen to this time?"

"Bloke down the Bull Ring's offered to Botox my G-spot."

"Pricey?"

"Bargain basement, Jen. The syringes are all second-hand, but he's happy to soak mine in creosote first."

"Better safe than sorry, Shel."

A free kick landed in the donkey sanctuary, triggering braying from the asses, and cheering from the players. The budget didn't stretch to a spare ball, so the bloke who had misplaced the free kick had to clamber over the fence and take his chances with the animals. He didn't seem happy about it and nor did the donkeys, judging by all the stomping and snorting.

"How's the wedding coming along, Jen?"

"Not so good, Shel. I wanted performing swans, a hot air balloon and six months in the Seychelles."

"Bostin, Jen. What happened?"

"I've got a male stripper, a second-hand bike and six days in Stafford."

"Oh, Jen. What went wrong?"

"Couldn't afford it. Gary's plumbing's up the spout."

"If the club paid our blokes more, Gary wouldn't need to spend half the week with his arms up people's u-bends."

"It's not like we haven't asked, Shel."

"What was their excuse last time?"

"Single-figure attendances."

"Pathetic."

"Their very word, Shel."

"I was so angry, Jen, I fell out of a minicab."

"I saw the pics in the East Bromwich Advertiser. Local paparazzi are a disgrace."

"There's only the one, Jen."

"Stu?"

"Got me to flash me minge. He told me it was for the final module of his media studies degree."

"Ooh, classy, Shel."

"Still, Jen. It's dead great you and Gary are gonna get hitched. He's a bostin bloke."

"He's got such a lovely speaking voice, Shel. I'll never forget the first words he said to me."

"What were they, Jen?"

"Show us your kidneys."

"Show us your kidneys?"

"I nearly fell off my pole."

"What were you doing up a pole, Jen?"

"Dancing."

"Dancing?"

"Upside down in a see-through thong."

"Jen! You never worked at *Spearmint Monkey*?"

"The tips were big and it's in a dead glam bit of Coventry."

"It's not a very romantic start to a relationship, is it Jen?"

"How do you mean, Shel?"

"You being arse-upwards on a pole and him shouting out, *Show us your kidneys!*"

"It wasn't what he said, Shel. It was how he said it. Beautiful speaking voice."

The AWAGs contemplated Gary's vocal attractions in silence, so my attention turned to the action unfolding on the pitch. A defender played a dummy to the opposing wing-back, who struck the ball with the outside of his boot and curved it back over the halfway line. A sliding tackle missed both the ball and the player in possession but created a trench deep enough for the Somme. The heftiest player tripped over the trench and went head-first into a puddle. He flailed about like he had been shot, until even his own players began to boo his theatrics. After an age, he got to his feet and swore at everyone, including the ref, who showed him a red card. He went ballistic and both teams joined forces to bundle him off the pitch.

Jen showed Shel her engagement ring.

"Is that diamond a real copy, Jen?"

"Genuine cubic zirconia, Shel."

"Must have cost a bomb."

"He nicked it."

"Bit of a cheapskate."

"Not really, no. He's on a suspended sentence, so he was putting his freedom on the line for me. I think it's dead romantic."

An Academicals player took possession and dribbled past two Athletic players before being scythed to the ground.

"Your Gary's just got a penalty, Jen."

"Hope he doesn't cock it up again, Shel. That South-West Birmingham Athletic goalie's a big fella."

"What's the score again?"

"7-4. All own goals."

"Gary got a hat-trick, didn't he?"

"Back-passing never was his strength."

The referee blew his whistle.

"Look out, Jen. Gary's running up to the spot."

"Come on, Gary, yer twat!"

"Boot it in their bloody net for a change!"

"Score and I'll shag yer!"

The ball thunked Jen in the face. She screamed and invaded the pitch.

Shel turned to me for the first time and said, "That's his best penalty this season."

We looked on as Jen headbutted Gary, triggering a mass brawl. I couldn't help feeling that they were all much better at fighting than football, and, as I watched the players, the officials and Jen flail around in the mud, inflicting injuries of varying degrees of severity on teammates and opponents alike, my heart swelled with pride. This is what it meant to be English. Twenty-two men had showcased their lack of talent with dogged determination for almost ninety minutes. Now, they were knocking seventeen shades of shit out of each other with a passion rarely seen outside of the honeymoon suite. There was such joyful abandon to the violence, and a real sense of togetherness. Everyone knew they were rubbish at football, and now they had switched to an older, less regimented sport. I felt so inspired by the unarmed skirmishing that I decided to join in: sometimes it's the taking part that's important.

RULE 3 - Violence Is Golden

Live fast and, before you know it, you've run out of time. Live in the moment and, at my age, all you've got to savour is rheumatism. But live in the past, and it gets longer by the day. Sometimes, I relive my regrets, revisit my blunders and rage at the eternal *if only*. At other times, I go easy on myself and reflect on friends made, fun had, and kindnesses shown. But what if you've invested all your energy into doing the wrong thing? Would nostalgia still work if you had spent your life breaking every moral code known to Man?

Finding someone who had done exactly that took many nights of meticulous mingling with the worst customers East London's hostelries had to offer, but eventually I hit the jackpot and fixed up a drink with the villain of my dreams. Everyone called him Carroll. I'm guessing it was his surname, but one thing was for sure: this was a man who knew where all the bodies were buried, largely because he had buried them.

I made my way to a London postcode that Trip Advisor described as "London's answer to Chernobyl". That might have scared off some, but I'm no tourist and people don't generally bother to mug a man who looks like he has nothing to steal.

Some pubs want to be found. Others prefer to lie low. *The Goodwill* skulked at the end of an alley specifically designed for murder and vertical assignations. Its sign – a Stanley knife and knuckleduster - swung in the wind like a gibbet, and dangling off the doorknob, a worm-eaten notice read, *No Guide Dogs*. The place smelt like an old offenders' institution, largely due the prevalence of old offenders. The décor wasn't all that: keys grimaced through a piano's shattered lid, a bald Christmas tree rotted in the corner and the pool table had been slashed with a knife, much like many of the customers.

The young barman was menacingly smart: clean-cut, pristine shirt, boxer's build. I ordered a Snakebite, Pernod and Black and "Whatever Carroll's having."

At that, the room went silent, like a gunslingers' saloon bar after someone's called Clint Eastwood's cowboy a prancing fairy.

Thirty-odd pairs of eyes watched the barman pour my lager, cider, aniseed, and blackcurrant combo and trace a skull on the head of Carroll's Guinness. As I'd suspected, they only took cash.

Even among The Goodwill's line-up of ageing borstal-botherers, Carroll was not exactly tough to spot. He had more scars than hair and sported the reassuring demeanour of a Chechen warlord; features hacked out of granite, bone-breaking fists, and a suit specially tailored for making threats in.

Carroll had two tables to himself and there was no one within twenty feet of him, as if his body generated a hermetic circle of fear.

He accepted the skull-topped stout but declined my offer of a handshake.

I took the seat directly opposite him, and said, "Thanks for agreeing to ..."

"Let's get this done," he interrupted in a voice as melodic as a laryngitic bullfrog's.

He wasn't here to listen. That was my job. Luckily, that's just how I like it. I supped my Snakebite and let him unburden himself.

"I started off in the early fifties as a bookie's runner for Guy Ritchie," Carroll began. "Golden years, they was - Soho was just a village. Violent, mind you, but friendly; full of villains and well-known faces, not Jack-the-Lads and plastic gangsters like it is now. These days, there's no respect, just no-value nonce cases, toe rags and pansified druggies - phonies and frauds who've never done any proper bird and who'd rather get a kick in the assets than slip an old lady a few quid for a new coat. But back in the day, there was Ronnie "The Hat" McVitie, "Mad" Reggie Frazer, and the Kray Triplets - the true Wellingtons of Crime."

As Carroll paused to sup the skull off his Guinness, I took a moment to marvel silently at the prodigious inaccuracy of his memory. Don't get me wrong, I hadn't expected watertight testimony from a bloke who had bent the letter of the law for decades. But this was *Absolute Bullshit* – a point modern science has identified as beyond plausible. Had his memories turned against him? Was he beset by a cruel, brain-mangling medical condition? Or was he just having a laugh? He didn't strike me as the humorous type, but the jury was still out - and this was a man who knew a lot about juries. I let him continue.

"I did my first job with Crippled Jim the all-in wrestler, a bit of after-hours window-shopping. We bought a crooked van rung with false plates in a slaughter down the Borough. Earned a chunk of money - fifty large in the bin. Broadmoor Danny was the brains behind the whole operation. You know the fella; he planned The Great Tube Robbery, which would have gone down as a bigger job than Brinks Mat if the escalators hadn't been out of order at Mornington

Crescent."

Carroll made a sound that could have been a laugh, but I wasn't sure. I did my best to echo it. He narrowed his eyes, as if he were taking aim at my temple through the sights of a Kalashnikov. It wasn't a relaxing moment, but I'd not come here to relax. I was here to unravel the secrets of another man's life. I wasn't entirely sure that that's what I was getting, but I wasn't about to argue.

Carroll narrowed the intensity of his gaze by a nano-smidgeon and continued, "When Broadmoor Danny done a runner with Norman No Legs, I teamed up with a gang of Hassidic Yardies and ran guns for Hummus, FETA and the RNLI."

I spluttered on my Snakebite. Carroll cracked his knuckles. I tried not to notice that his fists were tattooed with the words *Late* and *Hove*, but I couldn't help noticing that he had noticed my efforts not to be noticed.

"What are you looking at?" Carroll raged. "The tattooist was dyslexic!"

I raised a palm in apology.

"That's better," Carroll continued. "You wouldn't want to get on the wrong side of me. I ate my social worker! You should be pissing your pants with sheer respect." He gripped his Guinness like a Molotov cocktail. "Listen, I'm the kind of man who wouldn't say his glass is half empty and I wouldn't say it's half full neither, but if you keep looking at me in that tone of voice, I'll grind the glass into your throat."

At that, Carroll cackled like a cockney witch and leant in. "You know that robbery on *Crimewatch* last week. Everyone thinks it's me and they're dead right, it was. I'm dead proud of my reputation. I don't like other villains nicking all the attention, see. I stabbed one bloke's biographer to death with his own biro. Ghost writers, eh?"

He had another laugh. It was fit to scare the pants off a Norse berserker.

I couldn't copy the noise, and I had no clue how to respond, so I tried to head him off with a pun: "Violence is Golden."

It didn't work. "Are you taking the piss?" His forehead furrowed like a sheet of corrugated iron.

"Never," I replied. If I could have surrendered, I would have – but this wasn't a war, it just felt like it.

"You better not be," Carroll snarled. "I'm a man of considerable bollocks, I'll have you know. There can't have been a decent villain in Britain who hasn't asked me to plunge a mug for them. Fast Brian also known as Quick Eric also known as Puffing Patrick is a good for instance. He'd been marked down for being murdered. Now, this character, he was not pansified, or soft. He was a good class arsonist, but he was also a grass, so I paid him a visit. This no-value leery git was shitless – he lost two stone in sweat the moment he set eyes on me. I tried to calm things down by talking to him, but when I said, "I don't know whether to bite lumps out of you or tear your face off, but I'll be lenient. I'm going to rip off your head and shit down your neck," he got right saucy, so I plunged him with a corkscrew, banged his head on half-a-dozen steps, burned him with cigarettes, put him in a cold bath and tried to take his teeth out with pliers, but I needn't have bothered, he'd already died of fear."

"Poor guy," I observed, hoping this fate didn't lie in store for me.

"Poor? Poor!! Why are you taking his side?"

I had no answer, so I tried shifting my sympathy from the victim to the perpetrator. "Must have been tiring."

"What, dying?"

"No," I said. "All that murder. Arduous. For you."

He harrumphed. Not a conventional old man harrumph into his

chin, but a death-metal throat-roar of a harrumph.

"I don't mind a bit of exercise," Carroll continued. "Keeps my ticker going. But someone grassed and I got done. Now, my lawyer's so bent, he could knobble a Jehovah's Witness and he got the charge reduced to manslaughter. The trial was still tricky, even though I do have a good knowledge of law through my way of living. We objected to seventy-three jurors in total, but after that the judge objected to us. Bearing in mind my previous, eighteen years was a result, but I can't say I was celebrating."

Carroll glared vindictively into his Guinness. It was nice to take a break from his malevolence and have the stout take up the slack for a bit, but I hadn't come here to sit in silence.

"Must have been tough," I said. Sympathy was worth another shot. Sometimes, even violent psychopaths just need someone to understand their suffering.

But not Carroll. He gave me a "Bollocks to that," then continued. "When you're doing serious bird, you've got to stand your ground. One time, this Geordie screw gave me a few verbal words, so I knocked him down. He got the raving hump, called for help and three of them bundled in. I did the lot of them with a big lump of lead I found in the yard. The Deputy Governor comes up and gives me some old fanny, so I chinned him and down he went like a sack of shit. He kicked up murders; twenty-eight riot police stormed in, and it was a right tear-up, but I creamed the lot of them. That's when they sent in the Marines. Thought I'd give them the benefit of the doubt."

The Marines, right. What is a man to do when faced by ever-escalating fibs? I dithered for a moment between questioning his recollection and drinking more Snakebite, Pernod and Black. I went with option two and let him carry on.

"I was taken in front of the Visiting Magistrates in a body-belt, but I fucked them off, dived under the table and bit their ankles. The Governor came in with a gun and started making threats, so I said "Listen, you mug, I've got to pull the plug on you there." I chewed through the strait jacket, took the shooter off him, knuckled him in the kidney, found an iron bar and really done him with it. I felt much better then, even though they gave me three years in solitary without a mattress surviving on Number One Diet."

I doubted Number One Diet would win many Michelin stars, and three years in solitary was unlikely to help hone a man's social skills. I would have felt sorry for him, had it not been for the heartless violence he had dispensed and described in detail.

"I served my stretch in full," Carroll continued. "Bollocks to good behaviour. As soon as I got out, I fled the country for a bit and joined the Happy Valley Super-Duper Troopers, the Kenyan equivalent of the SAS. Best years of my life, until I got court marshalled for flogging counterfeit bravery drugs to NATO."

While Carroll took a breather to sip his Guinness, I took the opportunity to stretch out my legs. They had gone numb during the bit about the prison governor assault and cramp had set in, but I knew this was a delicate procedure that shouldn't be rushed. To avoid kicking Carroll's shins, I rotated my arse around thirty degrees in my seat and stretched my legs out to the side. They hit something human, but Carroll didn't react. I looked down. An unconscious man lay under the table.

"Don't worry about him." Carroll said. "He's a hitman. I should know, I hit him." He threw back his head and opened his raptorial jaw, cackling like a power drill and displaying a set of teeth that would have embarrassed a self-respecting badger.

Fortunately, I didn't have to look at the inside of his jaw for long because he was soon talking again. "I've been off the villainy for a bit, renewing my acquaintance with the upper world, so to speak. I've got a tech idea - second class email. Second class email saves a packet on data but takes three days to arrive. It's important for messages that don't really matter. I got a little import-export business too and a share in an English pub in Spain. And I'm getting a new venture off the ground - shoplifting over the internet. The customer e-mails me a list. I nick the items, then deliver them to their door in a stolen van. It's the future. Interested?"

There didn't seem any point pretending that I was, so I just gave him a "No, but thanks." Why was I thanking him? Fear. What insights had I gained from our encounter? Nothing reliable. I felt like I had binge-watched Netflix's entire Untrue Crime selection. But there was one tangible thing I could lay my hand - or foot - on, and it was lying under the table. Maybe this undeniably solid chunk of reality could help unlock something truthful.

"Can I just ask you one last thing?" I asked.

"If you must," Carroll replied.

"It's about the bloke under the table."

"What about him?"

"Is he dead?"

"Who's asking?"

"No one."

"Good."

"Who is he?"

"You wouldn't believe me if I told you."

"Try me."

"Why should I?"

"I'll get you another drink."

"Fair enough," Carroll said.

Once again, the bar went quiet as all the customers watched the barman pour my Snakebite, Pernod and Black, and trace a skull on Carroll's stout.

I returned to the table and put down our drinks. As I took my seat, my foot knocked against the recumbent man on the carpet. If he wasn't dead, he was doing a passing impression of it.

I took a sip of Snakebite, and prepared to hear something truthful, something I could verify.

"You want to know who's under the table?" Carroll asked.

"Yes," I confirmed.

"Right."

"Go on."

"You really won't believe me."

"I don't mind. Just tell me."

"You're sure you want to know?"

"Yes."

"Information's not always a healthy thing to have."

"Do I look like I care about my health?"

"Curiosity killed the cat, and all that bollocks."

"Just tell me. Please."

"Okay."

"Who is he?"

"Vladimir Putin."

I spluttered on my Snakebite.

"He's not as tough as he reckons," Carroll continued. "All that bear wrestling, judo throwing, and bareback riding. It's a load of old fanny."

I had sat here and listen to Carroll tell me about the Great Tube Robbery, the Kray Triplets, and his time as a bookie's runner for Guy Ritchie, and now he was telling me that Vladimir Putin was lying under the table. Somehow, the President of Russia, and former lieutenant colonel of the KGB, had sauntered over to the worst pub

HOW NOT TO LIVE YOUR LIFE

in East London and got himself knocked out on the carpet. Rather than relying on his million-strong standing army or the world's largest stockpile of nuclear weapons, the terrifying trillionaire had opted for a fist fight with Carroll and lost.

"That's not true, is it?" I asked.

"Go ahead," he replied. "Take a look."

I crawled under the table. The lighting left a lot to be desired, but I eventually found the man's head. I switched on my phone's flashlight and examined him. He had thinning hair and a moon-shaped face with pronounced eyebrows and piggy eyes. So far, so Putin.

When I resurfaced, Carroll, just said, "Told you."

"It does look a bit like him," I replied.

"It is him."

"But what's he doing here?"

"He kept banging on about some geezer called Peter The Great. Apparently, he was the Russian boss some time ago, and he'd come to London to nick all our ideas about shipbuilding, and Vladmir, he wanted to do a similar thing, only about crime."

"He wanted to nick our ideas about crime?"

"That's what he said."

"But isn't Russia quite good at crime?"

"Not good enough for Vladimir. He reckons his boys are slacking, thinks they could learn from some old school London villains."

"So, he dropped in at the pub."

"Just after lunchtime."

"Today?"

"About two thirty."

"Right." Maybe it was Vladmir Putin, or perhaps it was a wind-up merchant who happened to look like him, I would never know.

"Now I've let you in on this, you're gonna to have to help me out."

"Another drink?"

Carroll indicated his untouched pint and shook his head. I knew what was coming, but that didn't make me any more able to avoid it.

"You're going to have to help me shift him," Carroll said.

"Can't he shift himself?"

"What do you think?"

So, he was dead. Now, don't get me wrong. I'm no shirker and I've had my share of criminal convictions, but accessory to murder was a new one on me.

"What about the other customers?" I asked.

"They won't say anything."

"The barman?"

Carroll laughed. "His dad's a lifer. I trained him."

"Okay, so we're just going to carry him out of here?"

"There's an industrial mincer in the kitchen."

"We're going to mince Vladimir Putin?"

"I'll do the honours. Just be a good bloke and help me shift him."

Put like that, it seemed rude to refuse. The corpse wasn't particularly heavy and none of the customers raised an eyebrow.

Once we had safely deposited the corpse at the back of the kitchen, Carroll just said, "Be lucky," and I took that as my cue to leave.

On my way out, I noticed that something had dropped off the corpse. It was a gold star attached to a white, blue, and red band, a medal I now know to denote an elite "Hero of Russia."

As I made my way westwards to safer postcodes, I reflected on my two-pint encounter with Carroll. A man's memories are his own, and what version of them he chooses to share with the rest of the world, well, that's up to him. But when it comes to events in the here-and-now, the truth has a way of outing itself, and that truth can be stranger than the wildest imaginings of anyone on this sorry globule.

RULE 4 - LIFE IS LIKE A BOX OF FROGS

Four hours after gate-crashing the rugby club beer festival, I lost an arm-wrestle to a fly half. I bought him a pint and in return, he told me a secret: "When you die, you get to make one final phone call."

He spoke with the assurance of the expensively educated, but I thought it best to seek clarification. "You mean, if you're on a plane that's about to crash or you're on your deathbed?"

"I mean, after you die."

"Right." I didn't want to seem ungrateful for the information, but I did harbour a few doubts. "How do you know?"

He looked affronted. "How do I know?"

"You look ... alive."

"Thanks."

I thought about all my dearly departed relatives and acquaintances and wondered why none of them had bothered to give me a bell. Maybe I hadn't topped their phone-a-friend lists. I asked the rugger-bugger to explain himself and, after I agreed to sponsor the team's pub crawl, he was delighted oblige:

***

"It all happened after my stag do," the fly half explained. "Everyone got monumentally bladdered, and by the time we were thrown out, only three of us were still standing. We didn't want the night to end, but the only bars still open made us feel about as welcome as a dose of Monkey Pox. Then my mate Tommo had a brilliant idea: why not break in to one of those tree-swingers clubs and prat about on the zip wires? Now, I don't normally go in for all that team bonding malarkey, but it was my stag do, so why not?

I'd known Jonty and Tommo since school; both top blokes with everything to live for. Jonty had just launched a yacht-delivery app and Tommo's Insta was going Interstellar. Life was good, but that didn't mean we couldn't indulge in stupid stunts every now and again.

We shinned up to the tree canopy by the light of the moon. There wasn't a soul in sight and the night-time silence was only disturbed by the occasional rutting owl. The view wasn't great, due to the darkness, but we did manage to find a basket and a zip wire. I was the one getting married, so I had first dibs.

Jonty and Tommo cheered me on as I clambered into the basket and zoomed off. It didn't half shift! I was the fastest thing in the forest - completely in the moment, not a care in the world. I whooped my tits off; I'll tell you that for nothing. I'd never felt so alive, but a thunking great tree trunk had other ideas.

I had no clue how long I'd been out for the count, but when my brain got itself back into gear, I found myself in a wooden cabin decked out like it was about 1956. There was a juke box, a pinball machine, a dial telephone, and a dog-eared local directory. There was a gnarled oak door at one end and, at the other, an elderly chap drinking whisky and playing chess with himself.

I could only assume that the concussion was playing silly buggers with my brain. I blinked hard and often, but the cabin remained resolutely there. I checked my pockets – no wallet, no mobile, no keys. Maybe I was a victim of a mid-air mugging. It seemed unlikely.

When the chess player noticed I was stirring, he abandoned his pawns but not his spirit glass, and ambled over to my recumbent body. He had a bald patch across the centre of his skull and curly grey-black side-curtains over his ears. His bulging eyes were livelier than anyone's I had ever seen, but his expression was terminally unimpressed. His once expensive suit was worn to ruin, and his silk shirt was missing half its buttons. He took a few seconds to look me up and down, analysing me as if I were an inferior variation of the Sicilian Dragon.

"You are doubtless *wery* perplexed." The chess player's English was almost perfect, but the *w* was a giveaway.

"Are you Russian?" I asked.

"Russian?" He looked offended. "Your head must be *wery vobbly*. I am from *Latwia*."

I was in no mood to discuss the niceties of East European nationalism. "Where am I?"

Instead of answering, he took out a cigarette and attempted to light it. His hands shook so much, it was painful to watch. I've never smoked - couldn't see the point in curtailing my life for a lungful of ash – and looking at this chap, I was jolly glad I hadn't.

While he sparked up, I yanked myself backwards and hitched my torso up against the timber wall. The cabin felt too solid for a concussion-dream, but the fifties décor was unreal: "Am I back in

Time?"

"Outside," he replied, his cigarette now ignited. "You're outside Time."

"Am I dead?"

The man nodded. That was annoying. I had my own wedding to attend. On the plus side, I still felt alive. When I pinched myself, it hurt, and my limbs all seemed to work. I performed a series of basic experiments on myself: I could cough, stretch, stand-up, itch my scalp.

The chess player smoked and drank his way through my life-affirming mimes, but he didn't seem to be enjoying them. After a few minutes of my poncing about, he said, "Finished?"

I performed a series of star-jumps to irritate him.

He took a gargantuan puff, coughed his lungs out, then took another drag.

"Don't you worry about your health?" I asked.

"My health?" He inhaled the remainder of his latest cigarette. "It's too late for health. I've already had most of my organs removed – a kidney, spleen, tonsils, a lung, a hip, a knee. Soon, there will be nothing left."

In the circumstances, I didn't find his final words particularly comforting. "Where am I?"

"A deep dark forest where two plus two equals five and the path leading out is only wide enough for one."

"Is it in Hertfordshire?"

"You won't find this forest on any maps."

"Are we still in the physical world?"

"Limbo. The in-between." The chess player indicated the gnarled door at the far end of the hut. "When I take you through there, that's it."

I stumbled across to check.

"No!" His gruff shout stopped me in my tracks. "Touch that door and that's it – oblivion."

"What are we waiting for?"

"You have one phone call."

"A call?"

He waved his scotch at the dial phone.

I had never used one. The oldest phone I'd ever owned was a Nokia 5110. "Who do I call?"

"Up to you. You get a minute on the line. Try explaining where you are, and the call is cut off, along with your soul." The chess player grinned at my discomfort. "Just choose your call well – and keep it general."

General? How the hell could I keep it general? I'd just died. That was a highly specific and deeply regrettable detail. I thought about ringing my fiancé, but I just couldn't face it. She already knew I loved her, so all I'd be doing would be breaking her heart. Anyway, weren't the police much better at that sort of thing? They had all passed exams in breaking bad news. It occurred to me that I could do something useful – I could warn my friends not to use the zip wire. The only problem was, I didn't know their numbers.

I went old school and looked in the dog-eared directory. Personal mobiles weren't listed. I was stuffed – who the hell remembers people's numbers?

"You look perplexed, my young friend," the chess player said. "You *vant* to ring who?"

"Tommo."

The chess player didn't hesitate before giving me a series of eleven digits.

"And that's Tommo's number?"

"Try for yourself." He waved his scotch at the dial phone.

The chess player repeated the numbers as I turned the dial. Was he winding me up? Would I get through to some celestial prank line?

But after a couple of rings, a familiar voice exclaimed, "Hugo!"

"Tommo!" I replied. God, it was good to hear a friendly voice.

"Where the devil are you?" Tommo asked.

"I haven't got long," I said.

"What do you mean?"

"You're a top bloke, I value your friendship, but there's something important I've got to tell you."

"This is all a bit odd, old chap. Are you quite alright?"

"Where are you?"

"That's what I asked you."

"I can't tell you."

"Don't be a doughnut."

"It's the rules."

"You're drunk."

"So are you."

"Get off the phone, stop fannying about and get back up here."

"I'm not fannying about. This is serious."

"Serious? It's a stag-do after-party."

"Listen."

"See you at the bottom."

"You're already on the zip wire?"

"Wheeeee!"

"But there's a tr..."

"Aaaagh!"

The line died. I swore. The chess player offered me a drink.

"A drink? I thought I was dead."

"Doesn't mean you can't enjoy yourself." He handed me a double scotch. I hadn't seen him pour it. He must have had it ready.

I hadn't got a lot to lose, so I downed it. My last liquid supper - a nice, smoky malt. That taste was the last thing I remembered before waking up on the floor again.

A familiar voice said, "Hugo?"

"Tommo?" He was bang next to me, similarly prone. Across the room, the chess player was at his board, fondling a bishop.

"Bloody tree trunk. Stepped right out in front of my head." Tommo wasn't making a lot of sense, but I knew exactly what he meant.

"I tried to warn you."

"That ridiculous phone call? Thought that was some kind of wind-up."

"It was life-or-death."

"Don't exaggerate, old man."

"We're dead."

"Really?" Tommo looked sceptically around the cabin, taking in the décor and the chess player. "Who's he?"

"He's Latvian."

"Oh."

Tommo and I dragged ourselves up. I felt even woozier than when I'd arrived. Maybe there was something in the whisky besides alcohol.

"Hugo, old chap," Tommo said in a matter-of-fact tone. "I don't suppose you've got a clue where we are?"

"Limbo."

"Isn't that a weird Caribbean sport people do when they're pissed?"

"Yes, but it's also where we are."

"Oh. Bloody hell. A purgatorial cabin?"

"That's the badger."

"I see. Is that a juke box?"

Tommo wandered across the room and started examining the

selection of tracks on offer. "Cliff Richard, Perry Como, Pat Boone..."

"My apologies." The Latvian looked up from his pieces. "The *dewil* has all the best tunes."

"The *dewil*?" Tommo mocked. "Who the *dewil* are you?"

"That's immaterial." The chess player made a move that put his imaginary opponent in zugzwang, a terminal situation in which every move loses.

"Who's in charge?" Tommo asked.

The chess player turned his bulbous eyeballs heavenwards.

"Right," Tommo said in a business-like tone. "Enough of this nonsense. Are we dead or not?"

"Dead," the chess player replied.

Tommo jiggled his arms. "Then why on Earth are we intact?"

"Look, it's like this." The chess player sighed. "You go to The Beyond in one piece. The *vay* some people die – how *vould* I have a conversation with them? *Vhat* if a guy falls into an industrial mixer – I couldn't *wery* well talk to a heap of mince."

"No. Quite." Tommo slumped against the wall. "Is this the end?"

"The endgame." The chess player smiled.

"Can't we challenge you to a match?" I asked.

"Chess just keeps me occupied between jobs," he replied. "It is of no consequence."

"We can't play to save our lives?" Tommo asked.

"If you can't play to save your lives, you *vill* have *wery* little chance," the chess player joked.

Tommo swore under his breath. He didn't seem to be buying this situation at all. "So, all dead people come to this cabin?"

"This is just the local branch," the chess player replied.

"But you're from Latvia," Tommo objected.

"I live down the road," the chess player said.

"So, it's like a franchise?" Tommo said.

"There's no money in it," the chess player said.

Tommo glared at the chess player for an uncomfortably long time, realised it was not a wind up and slumped into a defeated hunch, muttering, "Some bloody stag night."

"It's not much consolation," I said. "But you get one phone call." I pointed at the dial-up antique.

"Who on Earth do I call?" Tommo asked.

"Jonty?" I suggested.

"But what about my family? My yacht app?"

"Just warn Jonty about the tree trunk."

"Oh, of course. Bloody hell, where's my phone?"

"Mine's gone too."

"Oi! What have you done with our phones?"

"They are not necessary," the chess player said.

"They jolly well are," Tommo said. "All my contacts are there."

"Your Earthly contacts," the chess player corrected. "You only need one."

"Well, I can't remember any," Tommo said.

The chess player recited an eleven-digit number without looking up from his board.

"How the hell do you know?" Tommo asked.

"He just does," I said. "It's probably some kind of death thing."

"A death thing?" Tommo said.

I shrugged, "Just dial."

As Tommo inserted his index finger and rotated the dial, the chess player repeated the digits.

"Jonty?" Tommo said into the dial phone.

"Tommo!" Jonty's voice was so loud, he could have been in the cabin. "What's happening?"

HOW NOT TO LIVE YOUR LIFE

"No idea," Tommo replied.

"That's helpful," Jonty said.

"It's not, is it?" Tommo said.

"No, not particularly," Jonty said.

"Sorry, old chap," Tommo said.

"No problem."

There was a slight pause. I would have interrupted, but I didn't want to break any of the chess player's rules and have him cut off Tommo's call and soul.

Eventually, Tommo came up with the less than urgent, "How's Trix?"

"Bonza," Jonty replied.

"Jolly good," Tommo said.

"Well, I'm about to swing down now."

"No!"

"See you in a sec."

"Wait!"

"Aaaaaaagh!"

"Oh."

"You didn't warn him," I said.

"I was about to," Tommo said.

The chess player offered us both a drink. Tommo downed his. I knew what to expect, but I needed a scotch and I'd given up caring.

When we came to, Jonty had joined us on the floor. I had no idea how much later this was; all I knew was that I had a worse headache than on my previous two awakenings.

We went through the same rigmarole with Jonty: *Where are we? Dead. Where's my phone? Gone. Who's the weird dude? No idea.* Then we proceeded to the phone call. But there was no one left to warn about tree trunks. Who could Jonty inform about our hat-trick of fatalities? A girlfriend? A parent? A sibling? He didn't fancy any of them.

Jonty looked at the dial phone in disgust. "How about FaceTime, Zoom or Teams?"

"No," the chess player replied. "Voice only. That's the rule."

"Why?" Jonty asked.

"Look," the chess player replied. "You're *wery* lucky to get this – you are among the first people in human history to have this opportunity. Before you, the grave has been silent."

"Oh," I said, "Just how long has this phone call thing been going on?"

The chess player gave us a full-body shrug. "*Veeks.*"

"*Veeks?*" Jonty queried.

"He means weeks," I explained.

"He's Latvian," Tommo elaborated.

"A trial period," the chess player explained. "*Ve vant* to see how it goes."

"We're guinea pigs?" Jonty said, disbelievingly.

"Looks like it," I said.

Jonty picked up the local directory and perused it. After a while, he smirked. "They've got sex lines."

"No *vanking*!" the chess player shouted. "This is purgatory. Have some respect!"

The chess player may have been a spoil sport, but I couldn't help agreeing that a sex line was an underwhelming choice for a man's one posthumous call.

After he had leafed through the directory for some minutes, Jonty said, "I'm going to give this one a go."

"What is it?"

"Helpline."

"Bit late for the Samaritans," Tommo said, despondently.

"Forest zip-wire company. Out-of-hours emergencies."

"What if it goes to voicemail?"

"Just leave a message," the chess player replied, impatiently.

"Does a message count as your final call?" Jonty asked.

"Yes," the chess player snapped.

"Wow, my final contact with the world could be with a measly machine," Jonty grumbled, before dialling the number.

The phone rang. We waited. The phone rang again. The chess player reached into his pocket, took out a mobile and answered, "Night Caretaker. How can I help you?"

Jonty dropped the dial phone.

"Your property." The chess player took our phones, wallets, and keys out of his desk.

"We're not..." I began.

"No."

"Why?"

"I hate people breaking in," the Night Caretaker explained, and showed us to the gnarled door. It didn't lead to oblivion.

***

The fly-half looked at my expression and laughed. "Got you!"

He had. There was no use hiding it.

"Fifth one this evening."

"But I guess he got you too."

"Who?"

"The Latvian."

"What Latvian?" He paused. "You don't mean you believed it?"

Gullibility is an undervalued virtue, and I have been blessed with enough to get a medium-sized nation through the winter. Surprising really, as believing a load of gubbins suggests a character well-disposed towards humanity, an optimist full of hope and positivity. I am not that man, and yet I swallowed the story hook, line, and sinker. Still, truth is stranger than fiction and I'm stranger than most. Maybe the best conclusion to draw is that events, true or otherwise, can be mighty odd.

RULE 5 - GRAVITY IS A FORCE TO BE RECKONED WITH

Gravity will take your loftiest ambitions and yank them out of the sky. And when gravity teams up with Time, you've got no chance, as one of the bravest men in Middlesbrough found when he turned thirty in mid-air.

I met the unfortunate bloke in one of those flat-roofed pubs with violence on tap and botulism on the menu. A sign read, *Pensioners Two Pounds A Pint*, which seemed a cruel under-evaluation of human life.

Establishments like this tend to welcome outsiders with clenched fists, but no one bothered me for the first hour or so. People often think that my face is already so beaten-up that there's no point making me any uglier by hitting it, and I can't disagree.

It wasn't until I'd sunk my third Snakebite, Pernod and Black that I heard the immortal question, a query that has resounded down the generations: "What are you looking at?" It was spoken with a Teesside twang, something akin to a Geordie-Yorkshire mélange.

"I don't know," I replied. "What *am* I looking at?" I knew from long experience that this exchange could play out in one of two ways: fight or friendship. It didn't much bother me which; the lad was as toned as a marshmallow.

He played for time with a classic, "You what?"

"What *am* I looking at?" I repeated. It wasn't a threat, just a question. Who did he reckon he was?

He waddled up to me and tested the resilience of the neighbouring bar stool with his humungous arse. "You want to know what I am?"

"I want to be able to answer your question and tell you what I was looking at."

"I'm the former parkour champion of Teesside."

"And what's parkour when it's at home?"

"Free running."

"Cross-country?"

"I run up buildings and jump across them."

"Any particular reason?"

"Because they're there."

This was the spirit that had conquered Everest, and I couldn't help but admire it. Personally, I have always felt more at home on the ground, and I am as likely to take up parkour as long-distance knitting, so I was happy to pay him a compliment. "Jumping up buildings must take balls the size of watermelons."

"They'd only get in the ruddy way," he smirked.

I was starting to break the ice, but now came the tricky bit. "I'm just wondering how you can dash up buildings when…" I fortified my resolve with a sip of Snakebite. "…you're built like a bouncy castle."

He slammed his fist on the table and regretted it instantly. It's hard to win a fight with an inanimate object. After he had sworn extensively and nursed his bleeding knuckles, he said, "I retired."

"Aren't you a bit young?"

"Thirty-one."

"All your life ahead of you."

"Not exactly."

"Just give it a few years and you'll see how young you were."

He took a long, hard glug of bitter and uttered one of the most morose statements I have ever heard: "It's my birthday." He sounded so miserable, he could have been saying *I've got cancer,* or *I just killed a man*.

"Happy birthday!" I exclaimed merrily. "If I get you another drink, will you tell me what happened?"

The ghost of a smile haunted his flabby face.

After I'd plonked a bitter in front of him, he clinked my Snakebite and began talking with the energy of a man half his weight:

***

"It was a year ago today. I'll never forget it. Everything changed at once. One moment I was one bloke. The next I was another bloke entirely. It was dead weird.

I'd been doing parkour since I was at school. I was no good at sport, not interested in lessons. I needed something to get up for and parkour did it for me. You see, life hereabouts is completely non-existent. Nowt happens all the time and most blokes need ... an outlet. You see, in Middlesbrough, no one can hear you scream. Risking death seemed like the best way of getting a life and for years it worked a treat.

I was as thin as a whippet and I'd run up housing estates, shopping centres, you name it. After a while, just one final frontier remained – the power station. I'd gazed at it for years, planning when to break in, and how to approach it. No bugger had scaled the bastard. I suppose it was the threat of death that put people off, what with the volts and the drops. Understandable, now I come to think of it, but back then, I didn't bother much with fear.

On the night, it was everything I was looking for. Smoke-shrouded towers spewed flames, industrial waterfalls roared, transformers buzzed with electricity. The whole place was alive - like a giant electric dragon - and I was Saint-ruddy-George going into battle. I'd lived in the bastard building's shadow for almost thirty years, and it was high time I conquered it.

As I free-ran up the floodlit concrete, I was shadowed by my mates. Rob's twenty-two and a half-decent free runner. I never had to worry about him screwing up, I just had to watch my back – he was a glory-hunter, ready to fill my shoes if I ever slipped. Liam was seventeen and a total liability. Keen as mustard, but next to useless. He put his heart into it, but he just didn't have the legs.

I used a *Danger of Death* sign as a springboard to vault over a barbed wire fence. I landed, did a standing flip, and launched myself at a concrete wall. That gave me the momentum to sprint along its side, with my body practically parallel to the ground. I was a street acrobat, see. I laughed in the face of gravity, took its ruddy pants down and booted it up the bum! I grabbed a gas pipe and swung myself up to the next level. I never thought of falling; I just thought of flying.

Rob followed me up with an identical swing, but Liam didn't make it. We were going to have to rescue him again, and these things are never easy.

I jumped back down, crouched, and Liam stepped onto my shoulders. I held his feet and stood up, then Liam stood up on me, like a pair of circus acrobats. Rob reached down from the gas pipe and grabbed Liam's arms. I then pushed Liam's feet up until he tumbled onto Rob, landing in a pile and tearing his trousers on a steel spike.

"Liability Liam," Rob growled, as he untangled himself from the youngster.

I didn't like Rob's attitude, but we had a building to climb, and I couldn't be bothered to argue. I repeated my wall-dash and swung myself up to their level.

Now, when you're running up buildings, gravity's not your only problem. You've also got to worry about surveillance. We all had form, and another breaking-and-entering conviction would have done none of us any good. I picked up a rock and chucked it at a CCTV camera. It totalled the lens. There was glass all over the ruddy shop, mind you, but I'd got the job done.

I hurdled a bunch of razor-wire fences, climbed up the turbine hall roof and banister-bounced up a fire escape. Rob followed, practically breathing down my ruddy neck. Liam limped behind us, his trouser leg a-flap.

I stopped to look up. Two industrial towers speared the sky like an insult. I was determined to take them down a peg or two. You couldn't hold me in - barriers were my pathways, obstacles were my launch pads, chasms were my bridges - and in no sodding time at all I'd led us up to the roof of the nearest tower.

Climbing a tower is one thing, but jumping between two towers is quite another – particularly when the gap is wider than the River Tees - and that was what I was about to do. I was so buzzing, I made Liam take out his phone and record a video, not just of the leap, but of the build-up.

As I spoke, Rob stood at my side, jostling for equal frame-space.

"The world's my playground," I boasted into the phone screen. "Why walk when you can leap? Danger's a friend – it reminds me I'm alive."

Rob barged in, ranting, "He might be old, but our veteran leader is about to do a monkey-vault, a cat-leap and a four-metre gap jump seventy-five ruddy metres above ground!"

At that, Liam flipped his phone into selfie-mode and said, "And it's his birthday in a few seconds."

Once Liam had flipped it back, I added, "Age means nothing when you're free!"

I fixed my face with determination, monkey-vaulted across a spiky grid, cat-leapt onto some flimsy guttering, then flung myself into the void. As I hit mid-air, my watch struck midnight. The second hand stopped and so did I, frozen in the sky. I looked down at the distant concrete, felt myself drop like a rock and, in my mind's eye, my life rewound.

First, my girlfriend reversed across our bedroom, covering her underwear, and speaking backwards: "Yadhtrib Yppah!".

I felt my fall continue, conjuring another reverse memory. I was small and standing next to my mum, leaning over my birthday cake. I inhaled four times and the candles lit up one-by-one as mum reverse-shouted, "Snruter Yppah Ynam!".

As I dropped, I recalled a midwife un-smacking my arse, and lowering me by my tiny feet, as she exclaimed, "Yob a Sti!".

My fall ended just before I reached the ground. No idea how, but I looked down at the concrete a metre below me, then seventy-four metres up to the point where my fall had begun. It was ruddy odd dangling just above the ground, but before I could figure out what was going on, I was bouncing back up, only this time, my memories played forwards.

The midwife smacked my arse and lifted me up, shouting "It's a boy!".

As I rose higher, I blew out the candles on my fourth birthday cake as my mum shouted, "Many happy returns!"

Then, as I got to around sixty metres, my girlfriend walked forwards across our bedroom, removing her clothes with a "Happy Birthday!".

Once I'd reached the top, my body froze again. I was in mid-air, my feet level with the second tower's ledge two metres ahead. Something made me look at my watch. The second hand unfroze from midnight and made a single tick. The tick was so loud it could have been Big ruddy Ben and the force of the sound seemed to chuck me forward until my feet touched stone. My body swayed, then I flopped forward onto the roof.

The tick morphed into a cheer as Rob and Liam celebrated from the tower behind me. Luckily, I didn't appear to be dead. I counted my limbs. They were still there, and so was reality. A different kind of reality, a reality with fear in it. And tiredness. God, I was knackered. All the adrenalin had seeped out of me. I clambered to my feet and turned back to Rob and Liam on the tower roof I'd leapt from. They looked like I'd just scored a Championship League-winning goal for Middlesbrough.

Liam waved his arms. "Legend!"

Rob punched the air. "That was the biggest leap in the North-East!"

He was right, but it no longer meant 'owt to me. "It was the biggest mistake of my twenties," I said.

"Your twenties?" Rob shouted in total disbelief. "They were less than a ruddy minute ago. Happy birthday! You've just made history."

"Can't I rewrite it?" I asked.

"Rewrite it?" Rob scoffed. "Just jump back."

"I don't do that kind of thing anymore," I told them. "It's too risky."

Liam had gone quiet. He's a nice enough lad, but he's about as sharp as a dollop of custard. He turned to Rob, and I heard him ask, "What's happened to him?"

"Bastard's only gone and turned thirty in mid-air," Rob replied.

Rob was right. I was a changed man.

"I've decided to retire," I explained.

"But you're stuck on top of an industrial chimney!" Rob booted the air in frustration.

My so-called mates simply didn't get it. I gazed at the gap I had just leapt across and shuddered. "I could have died."

"Never think about death," Liam warned. "That's fatal."

Rob slapped him on the forehead, but I knew what Liam meant. A split-second of fear can kill any free runner - that was all it took. And that was why I knew it was no longer for me.

"I want to be a living legend, not a dead one," I said. "I want to live life with a safety net - take up gardening, open an ISA, commute, learn the trombone, get to know the neighbours, maybe join a library."

Rob couldn't have looked any fuller of contempt if I'd told him I'd stopped following Middlesbrough and started supporting Newcastle. "You've lost your bottle, mate".

I wasn't looking for my bottle. I was happy for it to stay lost, but I didn't expect Rob to understand that.

I looked out over the Middlesbrough skyline and pondered the constellations. Maybe I'd take up astronomy. It felt like a safe hobby.

The only sounds were a distant buzz of electricity and Robert and Liam moaning about me. It's amazing how sound carries when there's nothing between you but air:

"What are we going to do about Duncan, Rob?"

"I don't know, Liam. Point, laugh, sod off down the pub? What do you reckon?"

"We can't just leave him there," Liam said. "I mean, he changed my life."

"You mean he weaned you off roller-skating," Rob said, witheringly.

"You called him a *parkour superhero* on Insta."

"Course he is, Liam. Spiderman climbs buildings, Superman flies up buildings and Duncan sits on top of buildings whingeing about his age. Face it, if he's a superhero, his cape's faded."

I didn't care what they ruddy thought of me. I just wanted to go to bed, so I shouted, "Can't you call the Fire Brigade or Mountain Rescue or someone?"

Rob shook his head. "There's no way I'm going to watch you being winched down by the emergency services."

"I've got responsibilities," I pleaded. "Pets."

Liam looked like he was about to burst into ruddy great tears. "I modelled myself on you."

"Then you're a moron," I explained.

"You've let us down," Rob complained.

"Then get me down!" I demanded.

We moped about in silence for a bit before Rob asked, "How?"

"Call my mum," I said.

"Look, Duncan," Rob said with brittle patience. "You've broken into a power station, scaled a turbine tower and performed a record-breaking parkour combo. Do you really want us to call your mum?"

"Yes!" I didn't hesitate. "Please."

Rob took out his phone and made a show of checking the screen. "Would you look at that? No service."

I wasn't convinced. "Liam?"

Liam checked his phone. His face brightened briefly before Rob elbowed him in the ribs. "No service," he said, without looking me in the eye.

"Must be the altitude," Rob lied.

I never took my phone running. I used to think it slowed me down. Now, I'd come to a complete stop, and it was looking terminal. No one was going to rescue me, and I wasn't going to jump.

I turned away from my friends and explored the roof of my tower. It was basically a concrete patio surrounded by sheer drops. Its only feature was a poxy brick structure with a door-shaped hole. Given that I was marooned, I decided to investigate.

"Anything in there?" Rob shouted.

"Nowt," I replied as I stepped through the doorway. My foot trod on air. I fell forward into darkness, grabbed the doorframe, and dangled into oblivion. My life was in my hands - let go now and my thirties would total about five ruddy minutes. Fear weighed on my fingers, loosening my grip. I screamed out in fury at my lost retirement, using the rage to drag my body back from the brink, and I flopped onto the roof in a reverse bellyflop.

"Think he's all right?" I heard Liam ask.

"Champion," Rob replied, wearily.

Once I'd recovered myself, I clambered to my feet and wandered back towards my mates. They just stood there, gawping at me, a traitor to my former heroism.

I couldn't face looking at them for long, so I gazed into the middle distance at rows of streetlights, minor roads, and interchangeable houses. After a while, I found myself asking, "Is this all there is?"

"What, Middlesbrough?" Liam asked.

"No," I replied. "Life."

"Life's got nowt to offer us," Rob said. "That's why we're doing this."

"But life's all I've got," I said. "And I don't want it to stop. Not yet."

Rob turned away in disgust. "You've picked a great time for a ruddy mid-life crisis."

"It could be an end-life crisis," I said, the reality of my predicament having just struck me like a ruddy baseball bat. "I'm going to have to jump back, aren't I?"

They didn't have to answer.

Before I leapt, I decided to recall the final moments I had spent with my nearest and dearest. First off, there was my girlfriend. Earlier that evening, we had been having a row in the kitchen, and she was cooking with violence. She'd plonked a saucepan onto a hob and hacked her way into a tin.

"Listen, love," I'd explained. "I'm not seeing someone else; I'm just running up a building."

She'd emptied the tin's bright red contents into the saucepan and stormed out, shouting "Selfish wanker!" for good measure.

After she'd slammed the door, I'd heated up the tomato soup, poured it into a bowl and sat down on the sofa to eat it. I'd scooped up my first spoon when my phone buzzed on the coffee table. It was my mum. I'd said hello then swallowed the first spoonful. My face flushed, sweat poured from my pores, and it seemed possible that I might explode. I looked across at the empty tin, read the label and shouted, "Chilli? Bollocks!" into the phone. This was clearly my girlfriend's idea of vengeance – a soup-sauce switcheroo.

I plonked down the bowl, killed the call, and poured myself a glass of water. I drained it in one, filled it up again, and slumped back onto the sofa, just in time to see my dog lap up the sauce. He'll eat anything, him – vindaloo, tom yum soup, jerk chicken – no matter how hot. I reckon he must have a steel gob. Anyway, he loved the chilli sauce so much, he polished it all off, leapt onto my lap and licked me in gratitude, practically force his tongue into my mouth.

So, that was it, my girlfriend's final words to me were, "Selfish wanker!", my last words to my parents were, "Chilli? Bollocks!", and my last ever kiss was from a Golden Retriever.

I shouted at the Middlesbrough skies in despair. "It can't end like this!"

The skies didn't reply, and nor did my mates, so I just stood there like a plonker.

After a bit, I realised that I was dead hungry. "My stomach thinks my throat's been cut."

"Want us to nip down the chippie for you?" Rob asked, sarcastically.

Frankly, I wanted us all to nip down the chippie together. But I wanted to get there by bus, not by leaping across a van-sized chasm between two industrial chimneys.

Liam delved into his coat pocket and said, "I've got an old pie. It's a bit flat. I fell on it."

"Flat's fine, Liam," I said. "You're a lifesaver." Ageing pastry would make a better final meal than chilli sauce. Maybe the kid had something going for him after all.

Liam lobbed the pie. It was a decent chuck. He really put some welly into it, but it fell short. I watched the pastry's seventy-five metre descent with dismay. Even from this height, there was something moving about its final moments - a pie becoming an ex-pie - and it seemed likely that I would soon be following the pastry to oblivion. "Bit of a lonely death," I observed.

"You've got us," Liam said.

I looked across at the sorry pair. It wasn't a world-beating consolation, but I knew I'd probably be best off getting it over with and leaping back.

"Come on, Duncan," Rob said, "Leap! It's self-preservation."

HOW NOT TO LIVE YOUR LIFE

"Or self-destruction," I replied, still not convinced.

"You used to love the feel of air beneath your feet," Rob said.

"I don't trust air anymore," I said. "I trust ground."

"Stop thinking about it," Rob said, "And just live in the moment."

"I'm not a ruddy goldfish." I was starting to panic. An inch or two out and I'd be bungee jumping without elastic.

"Want me to film it?" Liam asked. "You know, for safety?".

"In case the first leap didn't come out the way you expected?" I asked.

"As a fall-back." Liam held up his phone.

I muttered the kind of prayer people make up at penalty shoot-outs and took a run at the chasm. I got as far as the edge, teetered, and stepped back. "Nah. Can't do it."

"That's a relief," Liam said.

Rob looked furious. "Why?"

"I forgot to press record." Liam said.

It was hard to tell which one of us Rob was most angry with, but I'm pretty sure it was still me.

"Hang on!" Liam fumbled about in his trousers. "I've got a Curly Wurly!"

This was good news, but I tried not to get over-excited. "This time," I said, "Take a run up."

Liam turned his concentration up to eleven, backed up and sprinted across the roof of his tower, spin-bowling the Curly Wurly into the air. All eyeballs were on the confectionary's trajectory, like a cricket ball headed for the boundary.

I fielded it perfectly and punched the air. Liam whooped with delight. Rob shook his head in embarrassment. And I held the Curly Wurly like a priceless artefact from an Inca tomb.

"A condemned man is entitled to a last meal," I said.

"It's a ruddy Curly Wurly," Rob said.

"And some final words," I continued.

Liam raised his phone and remembered to press *Record*.

I'd not prepared anything to say, but the Curly Wurly inspired me. "Living life on the edge is fine. But if you look down, you might fall off, and I never wanted to die the dream."

While I munched the Curly Wurly, I noticed that Rob and Liam were making strange gestures. Nothing particularly insulting, but I was puzzled. Maybe my words were moving them emotionally, or perhaps they just wanted me to stop talking. If so, I wasn't ready to oblige – I still had plenty to get off my chest.

"I had a mid-life crisis in mid-air. It's not the best place to realise you're mortal." I savoured the next bite. "Now, all I want is a little more conversation and a little less action." I was mid-way through the bar. It was like a contorted chocolate hourglass measuring my remaining time on Earth. I took another munch. "I want to live slow, die old, but it doesn't look like I've got a choice." I was almost out of Curly Wurly, so I prepared myself for a last jump. "Running up this power station was on my list of things to do before I reached thirty. I've got a different list now and there's only one thing on it: death – eternal solitary." I took my final bite.

By now, Rob was waving like a drowning man, and Liam had stopped filming and joined in. What a pair of plonkers! I was about to risk my life for the second time, and they couldn't even watch properly. I shrugged, shoulders up, palms up, a full-on display of bewilderment. They pointed furiously, prodding the air like finger-boxers.

Something was clearly up. I turned around. The brick structure's doorway was no longer the void I had stepped into. Instead, it contained a hefty security guard and an Alsatian, both perched on an elevator platform – you know, one of those "dumb waiter" contraptions. The guard was a local bloke, probably an ex-squaddie, and he looked more bored than angry as he said, "Go ahead, lad. We're not jumping after you."

I looked back across the gap at Rob and Liam. They were cheering me on, just like they had when I'd jumped the other way. This was it. In a few seconds, I could be free running back down to solid ground.

"You won't have any trouble getting away, lad," the guard said. "There's only my mate Derek at the bottom and he's got his face in a Wordle."

Ahead, lay freedom. With one jump, I could avoid arrest, regain most of my mates' respect and be home before sunrise. Behind, lay a night in a cold cell and a couple of months in prison. It was a no-brainer: the guard had a lift. We descended together and I struck up a nice rapport with his dog.

Rob and Liam don't speak to me much these days, but I don't think we'd have a lot in common. They're still risking their lives, whilst I'm busy living mine. I'd never realised just how much good stuff was on the telly. After all those nights running up buildings, I had so much to catch up on – the soaps, local news, women's football. Food is great too. Even dead cheap stuff, like crisps. I wish I'd taken the time to appreciate it all when I was in my twenties, but you can't teach young people anything, can you?"

***

The retired parkour star finished the last of his bitter and eyed my empty glass. "Get you another?"

Three Snakebites was enough for most men, but I really like Snakebite, so I took up my high-flying friend's offer. We stayed until closing time, discussing his new hobbies - stamp collecting was probably the most dangerous.

Heroism is a tough act to maintain, and we agreed that if you wanted a long, comfortable life, you were probably better off watching other people do the interesting stuff. He would not have struck a stranger as anything special, but if you judge man by what he is, it's easy to miss what he once was.

RULE 6 - ETERNITY GOES ON A BIT

I once met a man who told me he was Satan's little brother. It was during a lock-in at a Somerset cider house and we'd both been drinking for a shade under eight hours.

Gerald had a weathered look, a local accent, and a modest farm near Frome. It had been a tough day: a dawn encounter with a Tamworth porker had left him face-down in a piggery and his subsequent dealings with The Dark Lord had brought Gerald's long existence into question. He had always felt overshadowed by his brother, and he couldn't help thinking that eternity was passing him by.

In retrospect, Gerald explained over our twelfth pint, joining the rebellion against God had been a bit of a mistake. He had only been a junior angel at the time and his big brother had led him astray. God had been quite lenient, all things considered, and instead of casting Gerald into oblivion and tormenting him with eternal flames, he'd dumped him in what was later to become rural Somerset and told him to keep his head down, stay out of trouble and evolve inconspicuously.

Life as an amoeba had been relatively uncomplicated, but he'd have given his amphibious years a miss – he'd felt as soggy as a used teabag. Primate life had its plusses - body hair was a boon and feeling his spine straighten over the millennia had been intriguing, but he'd hated the forest politics - apes could be very bitchy. Homo sapiens had their good points, but he'd preferred the Neanderthals - much less pretentious. The Ice Age had been quite bracing and one of Gerald's best mates, Tim, a decent spear-thrower despite his squint, had got himself refrigerated in a nearby cave. These days, people called him *Cheddar Man* and queued to see him. It would probably have pleased Tim, who had always been a bit of an exhibitionist.

After the planet warmed up, Gerald spent thousands of years as a hunter-gatherer in Selwood Forest, which had been ruddy knackering, particularly after he'd done his back in building Stonehenge. The invention of agriculture had certainly helped - it hadn't been his idea and he'd been a little slow to cotton on, but it had kept him busy for a few millennia. Gerald couldn't claim that farming had been in his family for generations as there had only ever been one generation, albeit a very long one.

Frome was far from fertile. Would-be crops floundered on a vast, unhelpful bed of clay, so he'd moved into livestock. Cattle had always struck Gerald as a little on the slow side and sheep were, in his eyes, no more than woolly maggots, so pigs, cleverer than most dogs and older than humanity, held great allure.

Gerald knew pigs and he liked to think that pigs knew him. In fact, he had a lot in common with his Tamworths. They were one of the most ancient breeds on Earth and had changed very little over the past few thousand years. Also, like Gerald, they had long snouts, pointy ears and looked a bit flushed.

Even though Gerald was millions of years old, his apparent age averaged out at about fifty-five. It moved in long cycles, dipping slowly to around thirty-eight and rising back to seventy-two, before slowly retreating again. Each year of ageing took several human years, so it gave other people the general impression that he was almost as susceptible to Time as they were, but no one lived long enough to notice the cheating.

Technically speaking, Gerald was a serial monogamist: he'd always wait for his wives to die of old age before starting new relationships. His current spouse, Claire, was just under halfway through an average human lifespan, so, with any luck, he'd have several decades to go before he needed to start looking for another. He wasn't looking forward to this - Claire was a cracker.

Gerald had sired over six hundred and fifty children – surprisingly few for a man of his vintage. His latest, Stephen, was a handful and today had been his second birthday. It was that fateful event that had brought Gerald face-to-face with his diabolical big brother for the first time in over three hundred years.

After his dawn-decking by the pig, Gerald had breakfasted on one of its relatives, swapped his farm clothes for something equally unfashionable, and set off for the bright lights of Frome Town Centre. His tractor was past its peak, and it was pockmarked by numerous unplanned encounters with pheasants, badgers, and fallow deer. The licence plate had fallen off and Gerald had scrawled the registration number on the chassis in mud.

After driving past a field sprouting stuffed bin liners, rusting machinery, and balding tires, Gerald joined the lane separating the hamlets of Inner and Outer Wallop. An ancient feud divided the two communities and Gerald was the only man alive who could remember who had caused it, partly because everyone else was dead but mostly because it had been him.

The warring hamlets had two pubs. *The Fat Man* at Inner Wallop and *The Thin Man* at Outer Wallop, so they called each other *Fatties* and *Skinnies* respectively, if not respectfully. There wasn't much to choose between the pubs. Neither had changed since World War One and both refused to provide food under any circumstances. Each pub barred the residents of the other hamlet, and when they were drawn against each other in skittles tournaments, they would do battle at a neutral venue eighteen miles away. Both landlords were teetotallers called Brian who despised each other and hadn't spoken for over forty years.

For budgetary reasons, the two hamlets shared a village hall, which was partitioned down the middle and had separate entrances. Entirely segregated pensioner luncheons, bingo evenings and slide shows were held there, and the two rival Neighbourhood Watch Clubs watched each other with considerable suspicion.

People were called *incomers* if their families had been in their respective hamlet for under four hundred years and, even though the area was virtually denuded of youth, the handful of teenagers maintained the segregation. They would sit on separate benches, buy cannabis from different dealers, and shoplift from the other hamlet's newsagent. After dark, they would travel to Frome or Warminster to steal cars and joyride against each other, making the rural night sound like a low-budget Monaco Grand Prix.

There were no streetlights in either hamlet, so the night skies had a remarkable clarity never seen in towns. This was magnificent for passing astronomers, but it meant that the inhabitants of each Wallop were always falling into ditches, stepping in knee-high puddles, and treading in cowpats.

Each hamlet boasted matching eccentrics. Outer Wallop had a Mrs Cozpissle, who ran beekeeping classes, and a Mr Cozpissle, who restored steam-powered tractors. Inner Wallop had a Mr Twirleigh, who kept owls and a Mrs Twirleigh, who housed thirty-seven homing pigeons in the loft.

There were minor differences. The owner of Outer Wallop's post office, general store and off-licence chain-smoked, whereas the owner of Inner Wallop's post office, general store and off-licence always served his customers with an unlit fag dangling from his mouth after being forced to give up smoking on medical advice. A visiting doctor held his fortnightly Outer Wallop surgeries in *The Fat Man's* snug but held his Inner Wallop surgeries under *The Thin Man's* dart board. Only Inner Wallop had an osteopath, a gentle soul who had considerably boosted his patient list by establishing an equestrian club to encourage back injuries. Only Outer Wallop had a water diviner, whose encroaching incontinence was threatening to curtail his career.

It was the day of the annual Wallop-on-Wallop Games, a series of rustic sports contested by the warring hamlets. The event featured cowpat bingo, shin-kicking, welly-chucking, ferret roulette, and bog-snorkelling. Gerald used to take part, but the skills he had honed over the centuries meant he won every time, boring himself and frustrating the other competitors.

Time passes more swiftly as you get older and when you're almost as old as the Earth, that can be pretty zippy. Some of the duller centuries had passed like seasons, but the last couple had dragged a bit, what with their industrial revolutions, world wars, and TV talent shows. It hadn't all been downhill, though. As he turned off Friggle Street and onto the Frome Road, Gerald couldn't help noticing that the town's streets were in much better condition since the 1757 Turnpike Act.

Gerald chugged past the sites of several Iron Age forts and the turning for Frome Market. He had been visiting the market every Saturday and Wednesday since 1086 in search of a bargain and was still looking.

Frome was the biggest, oldest town in the locality and there was something about its idiosyncratic streets and historical insignificance that appealed to Gerald. He passed the box-church plonked there by the Methodists the other century. Gerald hadn't liked them one bit. They'd turned up from nowhere and whinged about his hobbies. There was nothing wrong with bull baiting, cock fighting, and cudgel playing: much healthier than Space Invaders and Angry Bird.

Gerald parked his tractor behind the square where several of Monmouth's Protestant rebels had been hung, drawn and quartered a few hundred years earlier for annoying James II. The parking spaces were a little small for agricultural vehicles, so he'd bought two tickets to be on the safe side. Gerald had been cautious ever since his horse got clamped in 1871.

Frome had once been mildly famous for its stale beer and innovative use of human urine in the textile trade. But, although the town had more listed buildings than almost any other town in Britain, history had pretty much passed it by. Gerald knew how it felt.

The town clung precariously to the slopes of two hills and the streets were so narrow, vehicles practically had to breathe in to pass through. Their names - Hunger Lane, Apple Alley, and Leg of Mutton Lane - were not all that much younger than Gerald, and their cobbles took their toll on his superannuated legs. Even for a multi-million-year-old man, he wasn't in ruddy good health. Ever since he'd dropped out of the clouds, Gerald had been tormented by a variety of minor ailments: piles, eczema, migraines, kidney stones, asthma, diabetes, arthritis, and flatulence. Sometimes, he almost envied his brother – Satan only had to worry about the heat.

But Gerald had no time to complain; he was a man on a mission. He walked up Anchor Barton, for centuries a stinking accumulation of dunghills, slaughterhouses, and tallow melting sheds. Now, it sported shops selling pipes, cheese, and tourism, and a pub offering pensioner roasts. Whenever the staff doubted Gerald was old enough to qualify, he'd regale them with detailed reminiscences of the Crimean War, and they'd relent after the third or fourth anecdote.

Gerald found the toy shop he'd been looking for and bought his son a dinosaur mobile. He had found actual dinosaurs a grumpy lot on the whole, but these were all made of plastic, so it would probably be all right.

His task accomplished, Gerald walked past the pub in which he had inadvertently started the Frome Riot of 1832 and hopped back on board his tractor.

Gerald decided to drive back through Selwood Forest. He couldn't talk to its avian inhabitants, but he could read them. If rooks fed near their nests, rain was on its way; if they fed further afield, it would be sunny. If a raven perched on your house, you'd be rich; if it circled without landing, Death was on his way. But right now, a birthday was on the agenda, so Gerald stepped on the accelerator and took his tractor up to its maximum speed, twelve miles per hour.

Claire and Stephen were waiting for his return, and as soon as Gerald stepped off his tractor, Stephen ran up to Gerald, shouting "Upside down, daddy!" Gerald happily obliged and, while his inverted son dangled and giggled, he wondered what it must be like to be so impossibly young, to have a life spanning two years rather than a number adjacent to infinity.

But Claire brought his wool-gatherings to a close with the ominous words, "I think you'd better have a look at the back field."

"What's wrong, my love? Have them drains burst again?"

Her expression said it was more than a plumbing issue.

Gerald span Stephen upright and carried him round the back of the farmhouse on his shoulders.

"Daddy, look!" Stephen pointed across the field.

Gerald had seen crop circles before, but never on his own land, and where he was concerned, *never* was a very long time indeed. Gerald carried Stephen over to the mystery pattern and took a closer look. It was a fractal formation with a standing centre and a series of intricate grapeshot rings around its perimeter. The lay of the crop was also unusual, running from one side to the other, not spiralling like most other formations. The indentations were springy to the step, suggesting it was all freshly laid. Gerald had to admire the handiwork: everything was crafted with mathematical precision, every stalk was in place, there were no visible construction lines and the ground lay was superb.

A high-pitched "Dad!" snapped Gerald back to reality. He had got so wrapped up in the design's fiendish detail, he'd almost dropped his toddler.

Gerald steadied Stephen and gave the crop circle a final appraisal. To the uninitiated, it was an abstract pattern, but to Gerald, it was a message in a language popular before the Ice Age. It read: *Wotcha Lardy! Get in touch, Big Bruv x*.

Gerald groaned. He was going to have to summon Satan. It was a right pain in the rectum. He would have to dance naked in the woods, and Gerald had always been a touch sensitive about his weight and his dancing skills.

Once he had deposited his son with Claire, Gerald changed into a knee-length tunic and white hooded cloak. Gerald had never had time for druids, with their fashion crimes and drug abuse. But if he was going to get in touch with his big brother, he would have to go through the motions. Walking barefoot across Black Dog Hill in his pagan get-up, he felt a little foolish, but feelings can be deceptive - he looked extremely foolish.

Gerald couldn't help noticing that the ley lines were particularly pronounced that morning. Their orange glow stretched out across the landscape, and he could hear their buzz louder than a dawn chorus. Electricity pylons and mobile phone masts were mildly annoying, but they didn't make a tenth as much racket as these infernal ley lines, inaudible and invisible to all mortals but shriller than sirens to Gerald.

He found a secluded carpet of bramble with a thick oak canopy and began chanting a Latin incantation. He didn't know why Satan always insisted on Latin. Perhaps it was because he knew Gerald was the last remaining person to have spoken the language to Ancient Romans. Even so, chanting Latin made it near-impossible for him to keep in step whilst he performed the requisite ritual jigging.

After stripping naked, waggling his beer belly, and gyrating his arthritic hips for far longer than seemed feasible, smoke billowed and a weedy voice remarked, "Fab-u-lous!" It was Beelzebub, the fussy little twerp. Satan hadn't even bothered to turn up in person.

"Oh, Christ," Gerald moaned.

Beelzebub winced. "Don't mention him."

"Then go easy on my dancing."

"I deeply respect your dancing."

"Thanks."

"It's like watching a walrus fitting."

"Watch it."

"Satan sends his apologies. He's a little tied up right now, but he'd appreciate it if you could you meet up for some nibbles."

"Nibbles? What's wrong with a quick pint at *The Fat Man*?"

"This is Satan we're talking about." Beelzebub had a point. He went on to explain that Satan had booked a table at the poshest restaurant in the area and had done so in Gerald's name so as not to alarm the waiting staff. Gerald always thought his brother a right prissy ponce and this was par for the course. Why Satan would spurn scrumpy and pies in favour of wine and morsels Gerald never could divine.

"I don't think he's decided precisely how he'll be manifesting himself yet," Beelzebub continued. "But the staff are awfully good and I'm sure everything will go swimmingly."

"What's it all about, Beelzebub? Did he tell you?"

"I wouldn't presume to understand your brother, but, if you ask me, he's feeling a bit broody."

"Broody?"

"You know, kids."

At that, an entrance to the underworld swallowed up Beelzebub and Gerald was once again alone with the trees, his belly, and his bare arse.

Gerald trudged home in his druid clobber, flung on his smartest clothes (a battered Barbour, worn cords, and an old cardigan) and took his tractor off down the Vobster Road. He wondered what Satan would turn up looking like this time. He tended not to visit Earth as a fallen angel, as people often found the broken wings off-putting, so he could be dining with anyone from a traffic warden to a bare-knuckle boxer.

The restaurant was as poncy as Gerald had feared. The building was Georgian, which felt almost contemporary to a man of his vintage, but it was decorated in expensively "rustic" style. In general, Gerald knew where he was with rustic. You didn't get much more rustic than him. He'd been living in Somerset for millions of years, after all.

The waiter led Gerald to an expansive, comfortable room with a real fire, a hand-knotted rug and a stone-flagged floor. It was the sort of place enjoyed by precisely no peasants whatsoever in rustic history, and the other diners all looked decidedly urban to him.

Before Gerald had a chance to decipher the menu, an elegant young woman approached the table and asked, "Can I tempt you with anything?"

"Do they do pie?" Gerald enquired.

The young woman laughed alluringly and sat down opposite him. Satan was a twisted git. For the first time in Gerald's eternal life, he'd got a posh dining date with a glamorous young woman, and it was his big sodding brother.

Satan gave him a seductive smile and asked, "How are the pigs?"

"Fine," Gerald replied. "How are everlasting fire, darkness, and ignominy?

"Mustn't grumble."

"Beelzebub is still a twat."

"I know. I only sent him to give Hell a bit of a break."

The waiter came to take their order. This was bound to be tricky. It wasn't so much that Gerald was flummoxed by the menu's sophistication, it was more that Satan and the truth didn't really get on. As a fellow immortal, Satan could speak candidly to Gerald, but he was only ever able to lie to standard-issue humans. His compulsion to fib helped him stock up his stack of souls, but it hindered lunch. Satan could only answer the question, "What would you like, madam?" by ordering dishes his manifestation didn't like, meaning that there was a high risk of beetroot-and-turnip vol-au-vents all round.

Gerald wasn't governed by the same obligation to lie, so he silenced Satan and ordered the most expensive items on the menu: a half-cracked lobster, a char-grilled swordfish Niçoise and a bottle of Christal Roederer Champagne. When dining with the devil, you might as well push the boat out.

Once the waiter had retreated with the requisite obsequiousness,

Gerald turned back to Satan. God, she was looking beautiful. "Any good sinners recently?"

"Nothing original." Satan fluttered her eyelashes. "It's soul destroying."

Gerald and Satan discussed eternity for what seemed like ages.

When the food eventually arrived, Satan scoffed everything in sight whilst making porcine noises that would have put a Tamworth runt to shame. There was laughter and pointing for a bit, then the fellow diners and waiting staff froze. Not in revulsion: they just froze.

Satan's eyes burned, literally, and her voice dropped numerous octaves. "Thank you for keeping our appointment, little bro."

"No probs."

"Sorry about the manners, but as they say, "When in Frome, do as the Fromans"."

"That's not how you pronounce Frome. It has a hidden o, like room."

"But that wouldn't rhyme," Satan protested. "And there's no such thing as a *Rooman*."

"Not that I recall, no." Gerald remembered the Romans well. They were a pernickety bunch, and wouldn't have taken kindly to a stray o.

"Tell me, Gerald, have you ever counted your children?"

"If I did, it wouldn't take me long. Right now, I've just got the one. It's his birthday."

"I know. I've bought young Stephen a present. What I meant was, have you ever counted the total number of children that have sprung from your loins, if I can use an unpleasantly biblical word?"

"About six hundred or so."

"Six-hundred and sixty-six, to be precise."

Gerald's lobster fell from his lips. He'd read Revelations when it first came out and Satan didn't have to remind him of the number's significance.

"Look, Satan," Gerald said. "Just because Stephen happens to be my six hundred and sixty-sixth child does not give you the right to poke your cloven hooves into his life."

Satan kicked Gerald with her stilettos.

"There's no need to be like that," Gerald said. "I'm just speaking my mind."

"But is your mind worth hearing?" Satan enquired.

If Gerald had one principle in life it was that he always spoke his mind, so he repeated the statement, rather unimaginatively: "I always speak my mind."

"How very tactless of you." Satan sipped her champagne and sneered.

Gerald knew better than to get angry with his brother. It was what he wanted.

"Stephen is two years old tomorrow," Satan said, "And he is your six hundred and sixty-sixth child, so I'm afraid, old chap, I've come to claim him."

"Bugger off. You can be his godfather, but that's your lot."

"Godfather? Not a role to which I'm ideally suited, given that I rebelled against God and became his everlasting opponent."

"Uncle then."

"Not good enough. Running Hell is getting tiresome. I want to hand it over to someone new one day - someone young with enthusiasm and ideas. It could be a great opportunity for Stephen."

At this, Satan handed him Stephen's birthday present. The wrapping paper was patterned with snakes and apples.

"Thanks," Gerald gently shook the gift. It jangled. "What is it?"

"The keys to Hell."

"He's two."

"It could be his home."

"Much appreciated, but there's no chance," Gerald said. "He is my son. I love him."

"I'll play you at poker for him," Satan suggested with a devilish look.

"You've beaten me over eight million, four hundred thousand times."

"Fiddle?"

"Six million, nine hundred thousand and seven – nil."

"So, you don't fancy your chances then?"

"Go to Hell."

"Not yet," Satan said. "And when I do, I'll take Stephen with me."

"No, you won't," Gerald said will all the determination of a multi-million-year-old man, "I've thought of something."

"Golf?"

"The Wallop-on-Wallop Games."

"You're on."

Champagne, lobster, and swordfish were not on many pre-match menus, but this was the first ever metaphysical battle to be conducted at the Wallop-on-Wallop Games, and both immortal brothers were buzzing.

The contest had to be waged on physically equivalent terms, so Satan dodged into the Ladies and re-emerged magically from the Gents as an ageing farmer of Gerald's ilk. They could almost have been identical twins had Satan not made himself slimmer and slightly better looking.

The tractor ride was fraught, as Satan ruthlessly mocked Gerald's meek adherence to the Highway Code. Gerald pointed out that it was rule-breaking that had seen them dumped in Somerset and Hell, prompting Satan to call him a "girly swot".

The Games committee were happy to accept late entries, due to the dearth of early entries. The six other participants were all in their late teens and early twenties, but Gerald didn't fancy their chances. They may have had youth on their side, but you'd be hard pushed to find a more experienced or cunning pair than the immortal siblings.

Gerald was made an honorary Fatty due to his weight, and Satan was made a Skinny to balance the numbers.

The crowd was segregated on hamlet grounds. Brian, landlord of *The Fat Man* at Inner Wallop, led the Fatty contingent, comprising the owl whisperer, the pigeon fancier, the non-smoking shopkeeper, and the incontinent water diviner. Brian, landlord of *The Thin Man* at Outer Wallop led the Skinny contingent, comprising the beekeeper, the tractor lover, the osteopath, and the chain-smoking shopkeeper. But to Gerald, the inter-Wallop rivalry was irrelevant; the battle for his six hundred and sixty-sixth son was an individual contest. Whether they bagged the medal positions or brought up the rear, the highest-placed brother would win custody of Stephen, and that was all that mattered.

The opening ceremony featured a Morris dance and a folk song about incest, then the first event was unveiled: a gentle round of cowpat bingo. A field was squared into sixty-four and participants placed personalized draughts on a corresponding board. Whoever correctly predicted the deposition of the heifer's dung would emerge triumphant. It was a game of bovine-bowel chequers, and the atmosphere was intense, even if the action wasn't.

Gerald thought of Stephen's first smile, his first words, his first steps, and tried to will the cow into dropping its load on one of his squares. But the animal appeared constipated.

Inter-Wallop excitement built to fever pitch as the cow hovered over a square owned by a young Skinny, but the beast just stopped to moo.

This was shaping up to be an endurance event for the audience: pulses raced, hearts pounded, and the pigeon fancier was close to fainting. For Gerald, it was torture, and when the cow's rectum hovered above the epicentre of one of Satan's squares, he could have wept. But to his relief, the beast just mooed, paused for dramatic effect, and mooed once again. Satan mooed back. It wasn't much of a moo, particularly for the immortal personification of Evil, but it caught the cow's attention. The animal's head turned towards the Dark Lord, and Gerald realised just too late what his brother was playing at. Satan's eyes flared with flame and the cow emptied its bowels in terror. It wasn't just a cowpat; it was a cow mountain. Satan gave the air an upper cut. The Skinnies went wild. It was one-nil to Evil Incarnate.

Luckily, the next event was one of Gerald's favourites. If there was one thing he was good at, it was shin-kicking. His technique was like a violent river-dance, and he had all the rhythm of a seasoned Kilkenny prancer. Once he'd booted three Skinny opponents off their balance he stood shin-to-shin with Satan. It was as epic as Foreman-Ali, but without the fisting: perhaps Arsenal-Spurs would be a better comparison.

Satan mirrored Gerald's moves with uncanny accuracy. That was the thing about him: he did very good uncanny.

The mirroring accelerated, rival legs hokey-cokey-ing like pistons on a speeding steam train. Spectators from the warring Wallops were hypnotized by the immortal shin jiggery, which could have gone on until the end of Time, had Gerald not brought his river-prancing to an abrupt halt. Almost instantaneously, Satan did the same. This offered Gerald the chance to throw a punch. Satan dodged it, as Gerald knew he would, but the distraction allowed Gerald to boot Satan's legs away from under him and The Dark Lord landed on his arse.

The Skinnies booed, and their beekeeper protested that punching wasn't allowed. Gerald was fully aware of that, but the punch hadn't connected so it didn't count. Satan 1 – Gerald 1.

Welly-chucking was not a classic field sport: take the precision of the javelin, the elegance of the discus and the rotational technique of shot-put and bin the lot of them. It was all about heft and heft was Gerald's middle name. He employed the centrifugal force of his gut to dispense with the best Skinny tossers, then went welly-to-welly with Satan.

The Dark Lord's svelte incarnation lacked Gerald's girth, but his elevated wellies remained airborne for far longer than seemed natural. They were like rubber gliders coasting on thermals. Gerald could see that Satan was muttering an infernal incantation, but he knew he could never persuade the judges that the wellies were possessed. Satan 2 – Gerald 1.

Gerald was worried about round four: ferret roulette. The pocket scores - nought to thirty-six - added up to 666, which was Satan's kind of number. The Wallopers arranged thirty-six drainpipes across the grass like spokes on a horizontal wheel and placed a traffic cone at the hub. The cone contained a ferret, and its choice of drainpipe would determine the winner.

The eight contestants chose four pipes each, with the remaining four pipes reverting to the House. Gerald had honed his ferret-fancying skills over the course of many millennia and opted for pipes that were almost as weathered and pungent as he was. Satan favoured the most straight and true ones, which surprised Gerald, as it seemed completely out of character.

The spectators went silent as the traffic cone was removed and the ferret contemplated its fateful decision. Gerald could barely believe that Stephen's future rested on a polecat and a drainpipe, but God moved in mysterious ways - and so did Satan. The Dark Lord crouched at the aperture of one of his four pipes and, moments later, the ferret disappeared down it. Gerald's heart sank. If the ferret emerged, it would be 3-1: an unassailable satanic lead.

Satan was making ferreting noises, rubbing his hands together and beckoning the animal. A furry nose appeared, but that wasn't enough: Satan needed the full head. The Dark Lord crouched down to greet it, and the nose disappeared. Gerald could barely believe it. This was the greatest reverse-ferret in history. Satan's stare was perfect for inducing cowpats, but hopeless at enticing ferrets.

As it re-emerged at the hub, all eyes fell on the ferret. Gerald felt like a defendant awaiting the jury's verdict, and this was made infinitely worse by the certain knowledge that the sentence would fall on his son.

The ferret sniffed the air, lowered its tail, and bolted down Gerald's smelliest drainpipe. He didn't make Satan's mistake and kept well clear. The ferret de-piped fully at his feet and relieved itself on his trousers. Result! Gerald 2 – Satan 2.

There could only be one suitable climax to such an Olympian contest: bog-snorkelling. The tiny crowds were going wild.

Come on You Fatties!
Come on You Skinnies!
Who Are Ya! Who Are Ya!
Fat! Fat! Fat!
Thin! Thin! Thin!

The water diviner was practically wetting himself. The beekeeper was buzzing. The osteopath leapt up and did his back in.

Each Wallop nominated an immortal brother as their champion. Satan donned his snorkel and flippers. Gerald donned his snorkel and flippers. They both looked ludicrous. Neither cared. This was war.

The organisers had pre-dug a fifty-five-metre trench through their rankest peat bog and filled it with muddy water from the nearest duck pond. The quickest contestant over two circuits would be declared the winner. Rarely had so much ridden on a bog snorkel.

Gerald won the toss, which surprised him – he had expected Satan to interfere with the tosser. A whistle blew, a timer started, and Gerald dived into the bog. It was a dank, cold soul-destroying battle through murk. Conventional swimming was forbidden, so it was all in the flippers. Gerald employed a technique he had honed during his amphibian years. Satan had never had that opportunity; he had been busy burning in Hell.

At one minute, fifty-three seconds, Gerald's time was a personal best, but as he flopped out, he felt anything but exultant. His son's fate now lay in Satan's legs.

Gerald looked on as The Dark Lord plummeted into the bog. The flippers of The Beast were visible, but the rest of him was submerged, and the water was so impenetrable, he could have been deploying any kind of sub-aquatic tactic unobserved. Whatever he was up to, Satan was bombing along like Moby Dick in Speedos.

The Dark Lord emerged. Gerald held his breath. The judge announced the time: one minute, forty-eight seconds. The Skinnies went bananas. All was lost. Little Stephen would spend eternity in Hell.

Gerald threw his hands up to Heaven. There was no thunderbolt, but there was a complaint. *The Fat Man*'s Brian bellowed "That Skinny boy's a rascal. He was swimming!"

It was a serious allegation. Bog-snorkelling was all in the flippers. Swimming was verboten. The judge summoned Gerald and Satan. All eyes were on the secretly immortal adversaries.

The judge began by turning to Gerald, and asking, "On your honour as a Walloper, did you use anything other than your flippers?"

"No, that I did not."

The judge turned to Satan. "I'll ask the same of you. Answer on your honour as a Walloper, did you use anything other than your flippers?"

"No," Satan replied.

"So, there we have it," the judge said, "A fair result."

Gerald couldn't hold back. "He'll lie about anything."

"I will not," Satan lied.

The judge told Gerald that he had made a grave accusation and would have to prove it.

"Very well," Gerald said, "I will. Anyone got pen and paper?"

The chain-smoking shopkeeper ambled over handed him a notepad and biro. "I may be a Skinny," he said, "But let's make sure this is all dealt with fair and square. I don't want anyone querying my right to crow."

Gerald wrote a series of questions and gave it back to the chain-smoking shopkeeper. Once he had taken a long draw on his umpteenth cigarette of the day, he said, "Fair enough. Question one. Is the Pope a Catholic?"

As the shopkeeper was a human, Satan had no choice but to reply, "No."

"The shopkeeper gave him an old-fashioned look. I think you'll find he is. Question two. Do bears shit in the woods?"

"No," Satan had to reply.

The shopkeeper raised an eyebrow. "I think you'll find that they do. Question three. Are you a monkey's uncle?"

"Yes," Satan lied.

The crowd gasped. A flicker of hope hovered.

"Three lies out of three," Gerald said.

The judge turned to Satan and asked, "Are you a compulsive liar?"

"No," Satan replied.

"Well, he would say that, wouldn't he?" Gerald protested.

Things seemed to have reached an impasse, so Gerald said, "Right you are then, more questions."

After he had filled another page, he handed the next set of questions to Mr Twirleigh the owl-whisperer, who perused the list and said simply, "Golly."

"He's biased!" the Skinnies protested. "He's a Fatty!"

"It's all about the answers," Gerald said. "Not who reads the questions."

"Is this really necessary?" Satan protested.

"Yes," Gerald replied. "You've already lied three times," Gerald said. "That's got to be grounds for doubt."

"Very well," the judge said. "Go ahead."

The owl whisperer cleared his throat and asked Satan Gerald's list of questions:

"Is Donald Trump a Las Vegas go-go girl with more nipples than teeth?"

"Yes."

"Was Adolf Hitler a lesbian?"

"Yes."

"Did Kim Kardashian invent quantum mechanics?"

"Yes."

"Is Dwayne *The Rock* Johnson a weakling who would rather hide in a Wendy house than have a fight?"

"Yes."

"Is Elon Musk on benefits?"

"Yes."

"Are Frome Town Under Elevens a better football team than Barcelona?"

"Yes."

The judge blew his whistle and announced The Dark Lord's disqualification. Gerald had defeated humanity's nemesis 3-2.

After Satan had taken Gerald aside, given him a grudging handshake, and dematerialised in a grump, Gerald headed home to his wife and six hundred-and-sixty-sixth son. He watched little Stephen play with his presents, tucked him up and told him a bedtime story from the Bronze Age. Never had immortal man been happier, until he had a set-to with Claire about the dollops of peat bog he had trodden all over the shagpile. He'd tried explaining what had happened, but she hadn't believe him for a moment, and he'd decided to sod off down the pub.

***

Gerald's everyday tale of bog-snorkelling, cowpat bingo and Satan had climaxed, and we spent another merry hour or two sinking even more scrumpy. I didn't have any anecdotes of matching metaphysical magnitude, so we stuck to football and women.

Time is definitely a thing. I have no idea what it looks like, but its effects are rarely pretty. Gerald had more of it than he knew what to do with, and many of us don't have nearly enough. But whether it's long and wasted, or short and wisely spent, Time still happens.

And as for siblings, don't get me going. "Brother", "Bro" and Bruv" may pass for friendly greetings, but sometimes these can be the gravest insults known to the Brotherhood of Man. Just because you shared a mother or rebelled against the same god doesn't make you mates. For every happy Wright or Marx brother, there's a Cain and Abel. Blood's thicker than water and I'm thicker than most, but if you ask me, fraternal love is best left to the freemasons.

RULE 7 - TIME TRAVEL BROADENS THE MIND

I had been in one of Amsterdam's oldest cannabis cafés for a little under four hours when I got talking to a time-traveller.

"I'm from eighteen minutes time," the man explained through a cloud of Laughing Buddha smoke.

"Is the technology incredibly advanced?"

"A bit."

I checked my watch: it was three minutes past six. He was claiming to be from six twenty-one. It was not a particularly impressive claim, but I was intrigued.

Gentle questioning revealed that he was a Dutch postman named Ruud Moos. He spent his mornings lugging snail mail around the soggy flatlands of Edam, rimming its dykes on his cherry-red bicycle, and emptying his sack at assorted windmills and cheese farms. He was a practical sort of bloke and he liked to relax after his rounds by fiddling about with old motorbike engines, vintage televisions and odds-and-ends from car boot sales. One day, he was tinkering with a first-generation mobile phone he had bought from a gypsy and discovered that he had accidentally turned his shed into a time machine.

I couldn't understand why he looked so miserable about it. Wasn't this an opportunity to witness the most glorious moments in history: the heights of Ancient Greek civilisation, the wonders of the Renaissance, the scientific breakthroughs of the Enlightenment? Surely, he could observe legendary acts of heroism, feast his eyes on immortal beauties and gain inspiration from stirring displays of character in adversity. He could even solve the mysteries of the Ages – the construction of Stonehenge, the secrets of the pyramids, the assassination of Kennedy. And what about the future? Where would Artificial Intelligence take us all? How about inter-planetary travel? Nanotechnology? My excitement vied with my envy until I felt so conflicted, I was forced to roll another spliff.

Once I'd lit up a Lemon Haze doobie, Moos explained his predicament in a tone of utter dejection: "Every so often there is a Chosen Bloke and this generation, it's me. I'm destined to travel pathetically short distances in Time at inconvenient moments, crossing the space-time continuum in a quantum shed, powered by 1980s technology. I am the last of the Time Peasants. I am – The Lowlander."

Moos paused to pick something out of his hair. It appeared to be a small eel. I tried not to dwell on it, as I had a far greater interest in time travel than seafood.

"I mean well," Moos lamented. "But I stumble through Time, committing causality violations, creating predestination paradoxes, and triggering catastrophic butterfly effects. I helped a pensioner avoid a car clamp and that led the planet to the brink of World War Three. I prevented a football injury and that unleashed a plague of locusts across the Western Hemisphere. I resolved a teenage lovers' tiff and that reversed Evolution. I may be The Chosen Bloke, but I often wish they'd chosen somebody else."

I didn't want to cast doubt on any of this, but I do take an interest in current affairs and there hadn't been any locust plagues, global wars, or evolutionary reversals, as far as I was aware. When I politely pointed this out, Ruud explained that he had managed to avert these disasters before anyone had noticed.

"When did you first realise?" I asked.

"That I was The Chosen Bloke?" Ruud asked.

"Yes," I replied.

"It all happened in my shed. I'd owned it for maybe twenty years before I realised its time-travelling potential. Everything changed when I put this on my workbench." He reached into his postbag and showed me a breezeblock-sized mobile with massive keys and a tiny screen. I hadn't seen a phone that clunky in over thirty years. It was more like an item of furniture or a primitive weapon. "It might not have Bluetooth," Ruud continued. "But it's got built-in time-travel capability, the SIM card is made of Dark Matter and the battery is powered by an invisible web of cosmic strings."

I congratulated him on a seriously impressive piece of kit and asked him to talk me through what had happened.

"It was a Tuesday in early autumn," Ruud said. "I'd had a smoke and a pancake, then watched a documentary about Dutch mountains."

"Aren't the Netherlands flat?" I asked.

"It was a very short documentary," Ruud replied.

I was already finding his account unconvincing, and he hadn't even reached the time travel bit, but I didn't want to be unfriendly, so I said, "Do go on."

"I left my wife watching a soap and headed for the shed. It's crammed with vintage televisions, pre-war wirelesses, and early video recorders. I plonked the old mobile on a workbench and pressed a couple of buttons. The shed lurched and strange footage played backwards on the screens of my vintage televisions: mobility scooters reversed, burnt toast reverted to cold bread, plastic cuckoos withdrew into their clock-flaps.

I needed a dose of reality, so I opened the shed door and was about to step out when I realised that the shed was no longer in my garden, but in the infinite paisley wastelands of the space-time continuum. I turned back and slammed the door behind me."

I took a drag on my spliff. "The space-time continuum is paisley?"

"Surprised me too," Ruud said. "I'd expected something more ..."

"Inter-galactic?"

"Exactly. This was more like ..."

"A charity shop shirt?"

"But infinite." Ruud blew smoke out of his nostrils. "Where was I?"

"The infinite paisley wastelands of the space-time continuum."

"Of course," Ruud continued. "So, not long after I'd shut the shed door, my ancient gypsy mobile began to bleep. There was a message: *Contact Your Service Provider*. I pressed hash to see if anything would happen and a Call Centre Worker materialised beside me."

"A call centre worker?"

Ruud nodded.

"Literally materialised beside you?"

"In a sari."

As scenarios went, it wasn't the most convincing, but I hadn't come to a Dutch cannabis café for realism. "So, this call centre worker, what did she do?"

"Nothing," Ruud replied. "She just told me that she was my service provider."

"Your service provider?"

"Yes. Want to know what happened?"

I sensed that Ruud was tiring of my interruptions, so I decided to shut up for a bit and focus on smoking my spliff.

"So," Ruud began, "I'm in my shed, somewhere in the infinite paisley wastelands of the space-time continuum, and this woman has just shown up claiming to be my service provider, and I don't really know where to start, so I just ask her, 'Travelled far?'"

"Our HQ is in Mumbai," she replied. "But we've all been outsourced to the space-time continuum. Part of a cost-cutting exercise. Universalization, eh?"

"Not globalization?"

"If only it was."

"This is no ordinary shed, is it?"

"It's a faster-than-light flatpack."

"Wish I'd kept the receipt."

"It's not our fault that Edam's full of holes."

"That's Emmental."

"Wormholes. Edam's full of wormholes."

"Doesn't sound very hygienic."

"Hygiene's not the problem. It's the time-fidgets."

"What's a time-fidget?"

"A micro-jump to the Near-Future or the Just-Gone. Inconvenient if you're The Chosen Bloke."

"The chosen what?"

"The Chosen Bloke. It's you. Get used to it."

"What idiot chose me?"

"It's like cosmic jury service. Your name just came up."

"Look, I'm not from Sunnydale or Gallifrey, I'm from Edam. I can't slay demons or confuse Cybermen, I just deliver the post."

"Perfect. We don't need an Einstein we just need a Gump - someone who'll keep things simple and not try to change anything important."

She bunged me a weighty manual. The cover read, *The Panicker's Guide to Time-Hitches*. The space-time continuum is rather draughty, so I used it as a door-wedge.

She threw her arms up in despair. "Aren't you going to read it?"

"Can't you just give me the basics?"

"The basics are quite advanced."

"Well, I'm not."

"Okay, I'll get seriously remedial - the shed is for space travel."

"I can travel in space?"

"You can just about cross the North Sea."

"So not exactly Star Wars then. How about Time?"

"The Time bit is down to you. Sometimes, it's a random three-minute fidget, a surprise opportunity to re-boil a kettle. Other times, you can take a slightly longer trip and control it with your mobile."

"This antique?"

"It's an inter-dimensional space-brick."

"Couldn't be simpler."

"Nor could you."

"Thanks. What if I meet myself?"

"Just strike up a conversation. You'll get along fine."

"What if something goes wrong?"

"There's a Help Desk, but I wouldn't bother. They keep everyone on hold until they give up."

"Is there an app?"

"Your phone doesn't even do text messages."

She fiddled with my televisions, linking them up to an obsolete computer I'd bought at another gypsy funfair.

When I asked her what she was doing, she explained that she was building a chronological observatory. This would allow us to observe Time in the same way as an astronomer observes Space.

When she had stopped fiddling, there was a loud ping, and the computer's monitor filled with a map. Laser lines pulsed between the world's major cities.

"You're familiar with lines of Longitude and Latitude?" she enquired.

"I've done a bit of canoeing."

"Well, these are Lines of Attitude, supremely accurate pulses of Bohemian energy emitted by the world's most effete places: Paris's Left Bank, Tokyo's Fashion District, and – most reliable of all – Manhattan's Greenwich Village: it's got a seriously regular throb."

"Very rhythmic."

"I've got a precise fix on the Village's most Bohemian coordinates - a gay mime collective, a conceptual sculpture workshop and a nude poetry jam. This gives us Greenwich Village Mean Time – makes clockwork look irregular."

We worked together for ages, travelling a few minutes forward, a few back, always precisely measured by her Lines of Attitude and Bohemian Energy. It gave my life a completely new dimension. The trouble was, every time we would stream ourselves down one of Edam's faster-than-light wormholes, I'd get progressively more serious time travel sickness. Eventually, I had to stop, so I streamed myself back to when I had started, headed indoors, and watched the rest of the soap with my wife.

I looked at Ruud through my spliff smoke. How bored must a postman be to invent such a tissue of bollocks?

Then it happened. The front wall of the cannabis café collapsed, and a van swerved in. Its doors flew open, and its cargo of seafood flew across the room, showering us all.

As I picked eels out of my hair, I checked my watch: we'd been talking for exactly eighteen minutes.

In a sense, we are all time travellers, only most of it do it forwards in a straight line. The Lowlander was different, a zigzag merchant with a shed, an outdated phone, and issues.

I can't say I envied him. It wasn't as if I had any shortage of poor decisions to go back and correct, marriages to unbreak, crimes to uncommit, bottles to undrink, bets to unplace, or drugs to untake. But frankly, that does feel like a lot of work. My life is a linear catastrophe, and I wouldn't have it any other way.

RULE 8 - WAIT UNTIL YOU'RE DEAD TO GET FOUND OUT

I once met a bloke who had seen Bigfoot. He was a down-to-Earth mountaineering type of around fifty, and I had no reason to doubt him.

I was lost in America. My fourth wife was wealthy and wanted to get divorced in Las Vegas. After an Elvis-themed separation ceremony, I had stolen her Cadillac and gone looking for aliens in Nevada. It seemed the kind of trip best enjoyed stoned, so I had bought some skunk off a Hell's Angel. It was excellent stuff, so powerful in fact that I had missed the turning for Area 51 and ended up in Washington State's Snohomish County. No, I had never heard of it either.

I had stopped off at a diner and got talking to the guy in question. His name was Tom, and his story began almost thirty years earlier in his hometown. The place was tiny, remote, and surrounded by dense forest and misty mountains. It had a fraternity lodge, a grappling hook emporium, a timber yard, a church, and a Sasquatch-themed bar owned by Tom's father, Jake, a former baseball pro.

Jake was a handsome, roguish charmer, as barrel chested as Tom was whip thin. They were the same height and could have been the same person a quarter of a century apart. The men were as close as father and son could be, and when Tom turned twenty-one, Jake threw him a yard party.

Most of the town showed up and Jake was bossing the barbeque. He asked Jake what he wanted, and Jake replied, "A Sasquatch sausage."

"With hair or without?" Jake asked.

They had repeated this exchange at every family barbeque for the past decade, and Tom wondered whether they would keep it going for the next one. For as long as Tom could remember, Jake had been hunting Bigfoot. He would go off into the forest, follow tracks, lurk in his hide, and return many hours later – sometimes the next morning. When Tom was small, he had begged Jake to take him along, but he would just fob him off with wild stories about foul-smelling, fifteen-foot-high ape-men who liked to screech, yodel, and throw conkers. As Jake grew older, scepticism had set in, then embarrassment, and finally amusement. It was just one of those things that made his dad his dad.

Tom took his hot dog and mixed with the crowd. His dad's friends – the local cop, the pastor, a couple of loggers, and the grappling hook guy – all wished him luck on his big new ranger job at Seattle's Mount Rainier National Park and made familiar Sasquatch jokes.

Most of Tom's own friends had made it along to what was, for them, a bitter-sweet occasion, being both a birthday and a moment marking Tom's imminent move away from their shared nights of *Doom*, rooftop beers, and pointless dares. Tom's girlfriend was busy, but she'd promised to make it up to him later.

Tom heard his name called. It was his mother, Lauren, and she was gesturing frantically in the direction of his eight-year-old sister, Kitty. Kitty and her little friends were playing a tag game dangerously close to the shed where Jake stored his Sasquatch-hunting equipment. No one was allowed near it, so Tom scared the kids off with one of his trademark Bigfoot impersonations and they ran off squealing in terrified delight.

Jake knocked a couple of pans together. He was always going to make a speech, however much Tom wished he wouldn't.

"Not so long ago," Jake began. "Tom was falling off his tricycle, running about in a Batman outfit, and getting stuck up trees. But enough about his first beer."

Everyone laughed. Not so much at the joke, they just liked Jake.

"Now," he continued. "He's officially a man. Full of ... opinions."

More laughter.

"And maybe a little serious. But hey, he's as honest as the day is long and he sure has ambition. Now, ambition can be a great thing, but unfortunately, it's ambition that's taking him away from the greatest town in America. But you know what, he'll never forget where his home is. I can say that for sure. I give you my son, Tom!" He raised a can. "Please – take him!" After more laughter, Jake took a swig of beer and keeled over, sending a dozen Sasquatch sausages flying. A couple of people laughed, mistaking the fall for one of his pranks, but Lauren's screams drowned them out. Tom raced over, and helped the local cop try CPR, but Jake was gone.

Tom wanted space to mourn Jake in his own way and he wished the funeral had just been a family thing. But everyone loved Jake and his friends had brought along their friends, his neighbours had brought their neighbours, and there was an impressive line-up of retired baseball players.

Tom, the cop and two of Jake's former teammates, carried the coffin to the front of the church, then Lauren ran up and hugged it. Tom held her tight for a few seconds, then struggled to hold himself together. What should have stayed private was now public, and there was nothing he could do to stay detached. He attempted to prise Lauren off as gently as he could, but she just wouldn't let go of the coffin. It was painfully embarrassing. She couldn't just stay there all day, and he couldn't very well wrestle her off. As he was about to despair, Kitty scampered up, and hugged her mum's legs. Lauren loosened her grip on the coffin, and Tom led her and Kitty back to the pews.

The pastor's tribute was touching – Jake was a fine husband and father, and if the town had been big enough to have a mayor, he would have been our man. Jake was an excellent sportsman, a true friend to the community, and an enemy to Sasquatches. Come on, Jake would never forgive him if he didn't at least mention his hobby! Some guys take up golf or play bridge - but Jake was a true original. Sure, some of us may have laughed at his Sasquatch-hunting, but everyone's allowed a little madness, aren't they? And the world's a richer place for it.

The mourners retreated to Jake's bar. It was a strange place for a wake. Giant, inflatable Sasquatches stood watch from the corners. Bigfoot-baiting nets drooped from the ceiling. A variety of yeti portraits in impressionist, pre-Raphaelite and neo-realist styles lined the walls, and above the restrooms, there was a framed footprint the size of a truck wheel.

Everyone wanted to speak to Tom. Now the town's main man had passed, he was the focus of attention. Mourners expressed shock that such a lively, happy guy could pass before he'd even turned fifty. It didn't make any sense and there wasn't much else to say, so people made lame jokes about Sasquatches, with eighteen separate guys expressing their surprise that a Sasquatch hadn't shown up at the funeral. Other people wanted to know about the bar – was Tom going to stay and run it? Surely, after what had happened, he couldn't leave town.

There were lots of women Tom had never seen before. Plenty of them gazed at him. A few came up and remarked how much he looked like his dad.

Tom's girlfriend was chatting to a retired baseball player he half-recognised. The guy took Jake's Bigfoot fixation in his stride but was surprised to hear that Jake had settled down – he'd never seemed the marrying type.

People said they were concerned for Lauren, but almost no one wanted to speak to her. It was just too difficult to find the right words. She looked on the verge of tears, so Tom left a generous tab behind the bar and persuaded the local cop to lock up once it was spent.

There wasn't much Tom could say to his mum. They just sat on the sofa together and spent the evening watching game shows.

The next morning, Lauren woke early and seemed possessed by a surge of newfound energy, announcing that they were going to clear the Sasquatch shed. It didn't strike Tom as their highest priority, but maybe going through Jake's stuff would prove a comfort.

The shed walls were papered with forest maps festooned with coloured pins marking Sasquatch locations. There was a desk with a computer, a printer, and a fax machine, and beside it, a table covered with teetering towers of floppy discs, and piles of walkie-talkies, camera lenses and headphones. Over-stuffed cardboard boxes carpeted half the floor.

Lauren examined one of the boxes, then asked if she could have a few minutes alone. Her voice was so soft, and her smile was so brittle, it almost broke Tom's heart. He put a reassuring hand on her shoulder and headed out to fix the barbeque. Jake's fall had dented the grill and he wanted to straighten it out before packing it away.

It was a quick job, but he didn't get to finish it. Unholy, unformed words of anguish issued from the Sasquatch shed. Tom raced inside. Lauren was no longer the grieving widow, she was transfigured by anger. "Burn all this crap! Don't look at anything - just do it."

Tom waited for Lauren to storm across to the house, then turned to the boxes. If he did as Lauren said and burned everything, there would be no going back – the truth about his dad would be lost forever. He simply had to look in the boxes – he owed Jake that much.

Tom did not have to delve deep to discover that the largest box contained enough love letters and intimate Polaroids to seal a couple of hundred divorces. He gave the house one glance, then carried the box across to the trunk of his SUV. He returned to the shed and discovered that the other boxes contained nothing more than a chaotic library of Sasquatch sightings. These, he could burn. He stoked up the grill and began a cryptozoology barbeque.

A few minutes later, the kitchen door opened. The flames were leaping high, but it was still pretty evident that it was the Sasquatch articles rather than the letters and photographs. Luckily, it was only Kitty.

"Mommy's locked herself in her room," Kitty said. "Are we having a barbeque?"

"Not today," Tom replied. "Shall we go for a drive, give mom a bit of time to herself."

"Can we visit Bigfoot?"

"He might eat you."

"I don't mind."

"Okay, then. As soon as I've finished this."

While the newspapers burned, Tom and Kitty sang a silly song about Sasquatch sausages that made Kitty giggle. As soon as it was no longer possible to tell what had been barbequed, Tom damped down the embers and chased Kitty to his SUV.

This had to feel like an adventure, so Tom took them properly off-road. The car was up to it, but that didn't mean it was going to be a smooth ride. Kitty laughed as she bounced up and down in her seat. Tom smiled for the first time since Jake had died. They had to get away from Lauren's fury, and hitting the woods would do them both good.

Tom always loved the way light filtered through the treeline. It felt like the rays were alive, dancing on the windows. You never got the same effect driving through a solidly built city. He was about to put on some music when he sensed a movement ahead in his peripheral vision. He swerved as much as he could, then hit the brakes. There was a jolt. Kitty shrieked. Tom turned to look at her. She was sat bolt upright, staring at the shadows ahead. There were no grizzlies in this part of Washington state, so it was probably a black bear, and they tended to run away rather than attack.

"Don't be afraid." Tom put his hand on Kitty's shoulder. "Stay calm. Everything will be fine."

"Sas...qua...tch," Kitty mouthed in wonder.

Tom examined the most ominous shadow more closely. It might have had eyes, but that was about all he could say for sure. If it was a Sasquatch, it was a bit of a shortarse. Littlefoot, perhaps."

But whether it was Littlefoot or a little black bear, it was best left alone. Tom eased the SUV away.

"Sasquatch!" Kitty giggled. "I want one!"

"I told you I'd show you one," Tom said, gamely. "But I don't think it'll fit in the trunk."

The purpose of their drive supposedly fulfilled; Tom circled back home.

As soon as they pulled up, Kitty ran towards the house singing, "We saw a Sasquatch! We saw a Sasquatch!"

In any other circumstances, this would have been cute, but Lauren looked ready to cry. Sasquatches were a sore subject.

Tom took Kitty to bed and invented a story about a Sasquatch who went to school and became a cheerleader. It wasn't going to win a Pulitzer Prize, but it sent her to sleep.

Downstairs, Lauren lowered her voice. "Did you burn them all?"

Tom nodded.

"You didn't look at anything?"

"No. Don't worry."

The evening passed slowly. Lauren watched an old movie they had seen countless times before. Tom sat with her, until she fell asleep on the sofa, then covered her with a blanket. He made one final check on Kitty, then headed out for a drive. This time, he went through town, past the bar, and out to an overlook.

Tom watched the sun set over the Skykomish River, the jagged peaks of the Cascade Mountains and the distant city of Sultan. Jake used to drive him to this spot when he was small, and he had made a habit of returning whenever he needed space to think.

It struck Tom that there were months when nothing much changed. The weekday routines, the weekend rituals, the same challenges, the same comforts. But other times, there were days that life took you by surprise and flipped everything on its head. And when that happened, a man needed time to think. Could he still go to Seattle? Would Lauren and Kitty cope alone? How about his girlfriend? Did she really want to follow him out there, or was this the end of the road? And how about his friends? Sure, there were rivalries, resentments and flashes of envy, but he was the one that held them all together.

It was too soon to reach any conclusions, so Tom shifted his attention to the matter in hand. He took the box out of the trunk and carried it to the front passenger seat. There were hundreds of letters, and enough photographs for a dozen albums. It looked like Jake was seeing half the female population of Washington State. He clearly hadn't expected to die, so hadn't bothered keeping his affairs in order.

Jake really was the family man he seemed to be, but only in part. The rest of him was scattered between the other women. Tom couldn't figure out how Jake had found the time for them all. What with the town, the bar, the family, and all his Sasquatch-hunting commitments, there weren't too many hours left in the day. In one sense, Jake had been lucky. He would never have to explain himself to Lauren, at least not on this Earth.

As Tom drove back, it struck him that the town's lights were glowing brighter than usual. It suited the place, lent it a degree of warmth. It wasn't until Tom was a block away that he identified the true source of the light. He hit the gas, screeched to a halt, and threw open the doors. The Sasquatch shed was on fire.

Tom tore into the yard shouting, "Mom! Kitty!" No answer. There was no time to put the fire out; he would have to brave the flames. He wrapped his jacket around his head and prepared to charge in.

"Wait!" A female voice implored.

Tom turned. It was Lauren, just stood there, watching the Sasquatch shed burn.

"Kitty!?" Tom shouted.

"Bed," Lauren replied.

"Thank God!" Tom scrambled around for a hose and began to douse the flames. "What the hell happened?"

Lauren didn't answer. She just stared into the conflagration, transfixed.

"Did someone do this?"

Lauren simply smiled.

"What were you thinking of?"

"Your dad."

Jake had to pretend he didn't know why she was angry, so he said, "Dad wouldn't have wanted this."

"I know," Lauren replied. "I let Kitty have the Sasquatch map – she seems to like it."

Once Tom had drowned the last of the flames, he led Lauren inside and went upstairs to check on Kitty. She was on the carpet, facing away from the door and poring over Jake's map. Coloured pins marked a "Sasquatch Hide" and a multitude of "Bigfoot Hangouts". She hadn't noticed him, and there was only one way for a self-respecting big brother to announce his presence. Tom did the mother of all Bigfoot impersonations, a bloodcurdling gorilla-roar.

Kitty span around with a shrieking giggle. Tom swept her up, carried her to bed and told her stories about Jake's Sasquatch hunting. Tom had never gone with him, but Jake had talked in detail about Bigfoot fieldcraft and yeti-hunting gadgets. What Tom didn't remember, he made up, which was most of it.

Kitty was wonderstruck and, when Tom had finished, asked, "Can we see another Sasquatch tomorrow?"

"If you promise to go to sleep."

Tom didn't want to spend rest of the evening lying to Lauren about the letters, but he did want to keep an eye on her, so he sat in the lounge pretending to read "Touching The Void" while she half-watched a western.

The next morning, Tom was woken by a light but insistent knocking. Kitty was standing at the door, dressed for a Sasquatch hunt, and clutching Jake's inexpertly folded map.

It was ridiculously early, but Kitty was way too excited to go back to sleep, so Tom knocked together a substantial breakfast, and made up another Sasquatch story. As soon as the sun had risen, they drove off to Jake's main "Sasquatch Hide".

After twenty minutes spent singing about Sasquatch sausages, Tom and Kitty reached a fork in the road. One path read, "Rangers Only", the other led to Sultan City.

Jake had never been a ranger, but he was clearly no stickler for rules, and judging by the map, this was the correct route. They drove into the depths of the forest: branches knotted; roots curled out like tendrils. Kitty said it was spooky and Tom could only agree. Maybe there was something ancient lurking in the trees.

Tom tried to take Kitty's mind off the increasingly eerie journey. "What do you think the Hide will be like?"

"Hidden." Kitty giggled.

"You don't think we'll be able to find it?" Tom asked.

"It might be under something," Kitty said.

"The ground?" Tom asked.

"Maybe," Kitty said. "Or behind a big tree."

"It would have to be one wide tree," Tom said. "Should be easy to spot."

"I'll find it first," Kitty said.

Tom laughed. He was normally up for a game, but this was unfamiliar territory.

"We should stick together," Tom said.

The path came to an end around fifty-foot shy of the Sasquatch Hide's coordinates. Tom pulled up, grinned at Kitty and they hopped out into whatever adventure lay ahead.

Tom took Kitty's hand and, as they walked through the dense

foliage, their shoes crunched on the forest floor.

"See any big footprints?" Tom whispered.

"Sasquatches!" Kitty squealed.

"Quiet!" Tom hushed her. "You'll scare them all off."

Kitty giggled.

The trees parted, revealing what could only be the Sasquatch Hide. It was a luxury log cabin, and about as discreet as a cartel boss's hacienda. There was even a barbeque under the porch; an identical make to the fateful one back home. Even the dimmest Sasquatch would know that humans were afoot.

"Found it!" Kitty shouted.

"You win," Tom conceded absent-mindedly, as they walked up to their dad's so-called Hide. Kitty knocked at the door. She seemed to think that a Sasquatch Hide was where Sasquatches hid rather than a place Jake had hidden to observe Sasquatches.

Tom decided to play along. "Do you think Mr Sasquatch will open it?"

Kitty nodded.

After waiting a few seconds, Tom checked the door. It was locked, but only on a latch, which was easily defeated by a bank card.

Kitty skipped inside. Tom followed. It was a perfect romantic hideaway: the lounge had an open fire, a fluffy rug, and a mink velvet sofa. The bedroom had a king size and a ceiling mirror. It was blatantly obvious that Jake wasn't hiding from Sasquatches, he was hiding his mistresses. Tom almost admired him. An average guy excused himself by working late, attending fictional conferences, going on business trips or maybe taking a boys' trip out of town for weekend's fishing or golf. Jake had disguised his affairs by hunting Sasquatch.

Kitty was amusing herself by jumping on the sofa, and Tom had seen enough, so he suggested they check out one of Jake's "Bigfoot

Hangouts".

They drove for so long they ran out of forest. The location marked on the map was a suburban house, which didn't seem a likely spot for a Sasquatch to hang out.

Tom had his suspicions, so he told Kitty to wait in the car. She wasn't happy, but after he gave her some paper and pens, she agreed on condition that she could draw a Sasquatch.

Tom walked up the well-tended path and knocked at the door. No one answered, but there were voices within: one male, one female, both laced with urgency. After well over a minute, the door was opened by a woman in hastily arranged clothing. She looked at Tom, froze, then screamed. Tom didn't normally have this effect on people. He was the kind of wholesome young guy people turned to for directions or assistance with luggage.

While he was figuring out what to do, a sneaker fell out of the sky, missing his head by a couple of feet. Tom looked up: a middle-aged man was dangling out of a first-floor window. This was not what he had expected from a Bigfoot hangout, but as an expert climber, Tom always had health and safety in mind. He tried to persuade the man to climb back in, then talked him through the safest way to drop. The man fell awkwardly, but Tom's guidance prevented any breaks. Not that he was grateful; the instant he was upright, he scarpered.

Utterly bewildered, Tom turned his attention to the woman, who had stopped screaming, but had continued staring at him whilst repeatedly muttering the word, "Impossible."

Tom just said, "Hello."

"You're dead."

"I don't think so."

"You look just like he did."

"My dad?"

"Jake."

"Maybe once, Tom said.

The woman broke her stare and seemed to snap out of whatever delusion she'd been harbouring. "I guess it has been a long time."

"I'm Tom. Can I come in for a minute?"

The woman took a moment to recover herself, then led Tom through the hall. "Sorry about ... my friend."

"The friend in the window."

"He just dropped by."

"He certainly did."

They both laughed.

"We thought you were my husband," the woman explained.

"Sorry to disappoint you," Jake said.

"Disappoint?" she smiled. "You couldn't be better."

The woman made coffee and told Tom everything that was wrong with her marriage. Her husband was a workaholic gambler: whatever he earned, he lost. It was like being married to a zero sum. He was doing more and more overtime so he could become an even bigger loser. He was barely home, and she was lonely.

When the woman finally drew breath from the rant, she said, "You do look very like your dad," and "I do miss him," before putting her hand on Tom's knee.

Tom made his excuses and headed back to his vehicle. There was no need to visit the other Bigfoot hangouts: they were never going to be overburdened with cryptozoological primates. As he turned the ignition, he wondered whether marriage always had to be about deception and unhappiness. Did he really know his girlfriend? Did she really know him? He gazed out the windscreen. Maybe all love was doomed? He sighed, indicated, then noticed that Kitty wasn't there.

Tom leapt out of the car, scanned the street, and ran into the trees.

How long had he been gone? Maybe twenty minutes. How far could Kitty have walked? A mile, at most. Why the hell hadn't he locked her in? Kitty was a good kid, always did what she was told - why would she just wander off? Had she been abducted? Jake's stupid Sasquatch lies had brought this about. But this was no time for recriminations. He had to be systematic. He would cover a square mile and if he hadn't found her, he would return to the car and raise a search party.

The fields beyond the street were flat and featureless, so Tom headed back into the forest, maintaining a steady pace and shouting "Kitty!" every fifteen seconds. Speed mattered, but he had to take care not to turn his ankle on the roots – her fate rested on him. Panic now and he'd be the one in need of rescue. He simply could not allow that to happen.

Tom thought about Lauren, and how Jake's betrayal had made her a brittle, bitter shell. If something had happened to Kitty, there would be nothing left of her.

Tom did not have to search far before he found Kitty sat in a clearing. Relief flooded through Tom's body, then flooded out again. She was sat cross-legged on the forest floor with an eight-hundred-pound hominid.

Tom wasn't armed and he had no means of overpowering the nine-foot beast. All he could do was follow the advice he'd given Kitty with the black bear and remain calm, which was easier said than done.

Tom watched aghast as Katie handed the Sasquatch her drawing. The hairy great stink-beast perused it with care. Would he be offended? Amused? Would he even recognise his own image rendered by an eight-year-old?

The giant man-thing leapt to its feet and thrust the picture aloft, like a World Series trophy. It issued a growl louder than a pride of lions and performed what could only be described as a celebratory caper.

Kitty giggled and waved goodbye to the Sasquatch, skipping back to Tom. He hugged her and led her gently away.

Kitty grinned. "Sasquatches are nice. He really liked my drawing."

Tom never spoke a word about the encounter and Kitty's account was treated as a child's fantasy. But he never took the job in Seattle and devoted his days to running Jake's Sasquatch themed bar.

***

Tom had finished his story, and his steak. I couldn't help but wonder whether he had inherited his father's predilection for untruth. There was no sure-fire way of knowing, but Tom simply didn't strike me as the imaginative type. If you wanted a tree chopped, a cabin built, or a mountain scaled, he was your man. If you wanted an elaborate cryptozoological fib invented, you'd be better off asking someone who had done considerably more drugs.

Tom and his little sister had met a Sasquatch at their first attempt, but, for all his hunts, hides and hangouts, Tom's father may never have clapped eyes on one in well over twenty years. I wondered whether this was testament to the Sasquatch's finely honed sense of irony. Perhaps the humorous hominids had spent two decades dodging out of adulterous Jake's path and waited for his demise before making themselves known to his descendants. If so, I take my hat off to them.

Say what you like about Americans, but they live in one hell of a country.

RULE 9 - LOVE IS BLIND DRUNK

Long after my seventh ex-wife's wedding had degenerated into fights and fumbles, I got talking to the pianist. He was a fine-looking fellow, and no more than thirty, but his world-beaten expression suggested he had lived more than was good for him.

The piano's rack didn't hold a score, it supported a sketch pad, and he would consult this at frequent intervals. I wondered whether it contained some advanced form of musical notation, but closer inspection revealed it to be one of the most childishly inept drawings I had encountered outside a kindergarten: a shoal of bemused mermaids watched a herd of embarrassed elephants bathe in a moonlit lagoon whilst nude women queued to use a beach-side diving board. It was a work of art so poor in both conception and execution, it would have shamed a chimp.

"Nice pic," I observed, by way of breaking the ice.

"It might not look like much," the pianist explained. "But it sounds great."

I couldn't disagree. His tunes had been the wedding's only highlight. I congratulated him on his virtuosity and asked his permission to peruse the pad. It didn't disappoint: a poodle played Russian Roulette with a water pistol, bearded cherubs drank pints, pixies Morris danced to an audience of cross-eyed woodland creatures. The collection could have been composed by a committee of the ungifted after they had got drunk on meths and hit the crayons.

I returned his pad to the rack. "Well, you've certainly got something."

"Really?" His eyes lit up.

"Maybe a disease."

The pianist laughed. I poured him a scotch from an unattended bottle, and we chinked a toast to his sketch.

"It's just a thing." He shrugged. "I see sound."

People tell me a lot of things, but this was a first. "What does it look like?"

"This." He indicated the lagoon sketch, smiled ruefully, and told me that he had once drawn a Platinum-selling album. It was quite a claim for a guy headlining weddings, so I asked him to elaborate.

"I didn't make a penny from the songs I drew," he explained. "But I did date the lead singer for a few years."

The singer in question was an Irish rock diva named Donna, mostly memorable for her leather catsuit, fragile voice and even more fragile ego. Her apoplectic fury at a novelty cover version of her hit, *Little Man*, had made headlines. I didn't entirely blame her: it had been performed by puppet leprechauns in Santa Claus outfits.

"Quite a lady," I recalled, tactfully.

"I thought she was the love of my life."

"I've had a few of those."

"I gave her all I had." The pianist sank his scotch. "My time, my talent - I even gave her regular surprises."

"How regular?"

"Every other week. Tuesdays mostly."

I poured him another scotch. The wedding guests didn't seem to care that he had stopped playing; their attentions were focused on the mass brawl, currently tumbling out to the car park.

"So, how come you didn't make any money from the platinum album?"

"Song-drawers aren't songwriters – we can't claim royalties."

"And you've been playing weddings ever since?"

"Only recently. I used to have a career as a vocal coach, teaching women to sing. Younger ones, mostly."

"A singing teacher? Is there much call for that?"

"Among certain women, yes. I was good and they were grateful – often, too grateful - but I never betrayed Donna. I'd tell them I'd been with her for years and that would only make it worse. They'd say things like: *You're so stable. I'd like to push you 'til you wobble* and *Just because you've already ordered doesn't mean you can't look at the menu*. Women seemed to find my fidelity a turn-on."

Life is nothing if not paradoxical. The bride and groom were on the dance floor, wrestling. She had him in a neck-lock and he was close to submission. I thought about the vows I had seen them exchange earlier in the day: *To have and to hold*. Well, she certainly seemed to have him in a hold.

I turned back to the pianist and asked him how things had played out with the catsuit sporting Irishwoman.

"I felt completely secure in my relationship with Donna," he said. "Right up until the moment she dumped me over a pair of *Screaming Orgasms*."

I knew the cocktail. It wasn't my favourite. I encouraged him to flesh out the scene.

He agreed and began his sorry story:

"We were drinking these Baileys, vodka, and amaretto concoctions in some bar, when Donna told me it was over. She wanted to tour Norway with a band, and I wasn't welcome to tag along."

I started whingeing, "But I'm loyal, I'm devoted..."

"You're dumped," Donna interrupted. "Why can't you behave like a real musician?"

"I will if you want me to."

"You're obedient too!" She was practically screaming. "I despise conformists."

She left and I got drunk – not on Screaming Orgasms, I was feeling anti-climactic. After my ninth bitter, a customer took pity on me, lodged a cigarette in my mouth and lit it. I coughed uncontrollably, as I didn't smoke, but it was a thoughtful gesture.

For days, I moped about in my pants, sporting a never-ending stare. One time, I lifted a coffee and missed my face. Another, I put my back out lifting a croissant. When I returned to work, I told the women who had propositioned me that I was available, but they'd just say things like *Where's the challenge in seducing a desperate single guy? If I ever need a puppy, I'll go to the pet shop,* and *Get lost - you're too bloody attainable.*

Eventually, I got over myself and tried to draw some more songs. I crayoned with intense fury. Bins filled with torn pictures until I finally had what I was looking for: sunset over a crazy golf course as a one-legged angel putted against Elvis Presley. This was it! I took it to the piano, placed it in the rack and played the best tune of my life. Donna was history and I had a new song. Things were looking up.

I went off to see a mate in the music biz. Jez uses a wheelchair, but he's a mean drummer and an even meaner fighter. He was rehearsing with a bored session guitarist, and that perma-wasted vocalist who used to be in *Vague Alien*.

They were halfway through a track called *The Skeletons Are Confused* when the vocalist stopped singing, burst into tears, and dropped to the carpet. Jez wheeled over to console him.

The vocalist was in bits. "Do you think my car's lonely?"

"Where's it parked?" Jez asked.

"The supermarket," the vocalist replied.

"It'll be fine there," Jez said. "The vehicles are very friendly."

The vocalist stopped crying.

The guitarist jabbed a finger at the wall clock. "Ready to get on with it?"

The vocalist wasn't. "I need a bit of time to ... you know ... think about who I am."

I'd seen Jez lose his patience and set about people with heavy objects, but this time, he was a model of restraint. "Sure," he said. "You get your head together."

"That could take decades," the guitarist protested. "I can't go past six. Hospital appointment."

"Lobotomist missed a bit, did he?" This was the Jez I knew and loved.

The guitarist looked monumentally affronted. "It's for my son."

The band abandoned the session, and I took Jez to the pub.

"What a twat!" he began.

"The vocalist?" I asked.

"The guitarist," he replied.

"You can't blame him for going to hospital with his son," I reasoned.

"I can," Jez replied. "He doesn't have any children. He's just a lazy, lying bastard."

Jez was pleased to hear about the new song, but when I explained my personal situation, he looked totally bemused. "Let me get this right, you're asking a drummer for advice?"

"It's fair to say I'm desperate."

"I've got enough problems of my own right now. The neighbour's started monitoring my drumming with a seismograph. I mean, get a life! I never practice after eleven in the morning."

"But you do start at midnight."

Jez knew I was right, but that didn't stop him glaring at me for five seconds flat before he said, "Where were we? Ah, yes, you were asking a divorced drummer for advice about women."

"I was, wasn't I? Well, when I was going out with Donna, women were throwing themselves at me. Now I'm single, they're not interested."

"You're a free man. Don't go looking for another cage."

We sat in silence for a couple of minutes. I was beginning to regret asking Jez for advice when he had a eureka moment. He slapped the table with his palm and said, "If that lazy guitarist has an imaginary child, why shouldn't you have an imaginary wife?"

"And have imaginary sex with her?"

"Or have real sex with the kinds of women who fancied you when you were with Donna."

"Real sex, imaginary adultery?"

"Exactly!"

The first step was to learn how to be a husband. Jez took me for a training session in Muswell Hill and showed me an array of soul-sapped men in tow to wives and children.

"Look and learn," Jez instructed. "For them, life's adventure's over, fashion's a memory, weekends are for jobs around the house. You've got to get the psychology right - think garden centres, DIY, and superstores."

Once I had mastered that mind-set, Jez took me to a jeweller, explaining that "Even an imaginary wife wouldn't let her husband go around ringless."

The jeweller said we made a lovely couple. I bought the cheapest ring and left.

We headed for the nearest greasy spoon and set about designing my imaginary wife. It seemed best if she were a workaholic with numerous hobbies, leaving me at a loose end most weekday evenings.

As Jez riffed on my imaginary wife's personal attributes; I started to sketch her. "She's not who you thought she was," Jez explained. "She's become cold, distant, and however hard you try you just can't get her to understand you. It makes you sad – you are a romantic type, and you did once carry a torch for her, but now it's just really, really sad."

I showed Jez my sketch. My imaginary spouse had the right number of limbs, but that was probably the best that could be said for her.

"No one looks like that," Jez observed, accurately.

"That's just what she sounds like," I explained.

Once we had sunk a couple of bacon butties, we ran through the lies a few more times, until Jez said, "Okay, enough preparation. Convince me."

"I've been married for seven years," I began, uncertainly. "I am incomprehensible to my missus and in urgent need of several intensive sessions of understanding."

"Sounds like you're reading an autocue! You're going to have to learn to improvise. Bullshit is like jazz."

"I always though jazz was bullshit."

"Same difference."

I gave it a go. "We met on the internet...It was love at first sight... It's been a whirlwind romance ever since school."

Jez despaired and wished me luck.

The next day, I put out a few ads for new clients. *Singing lessons - 1-on-1 tuition*; *Find your voice - intimate instruction*, and even *Music is the food of love – come and have a nibble*.

It worked a treat, and my diary was soon clogged with clients. The first was a young Kiwi woman called Kerry, who trudged listlessly through her lesson, but came to life as soon as she clocked my wedding ring. "When did you decide to tie the noose?"

After I'd lied about my non-existent wife and whinged about our failing marriage, she said, "I'll bet you're rampantly monogamous."

I told her that there was only one way to find out – and we did.

Another client was a hyperactive Anglo-Indian called Meena. She raced through all her arpeggios so quickly we had time to sit on the sofa and chat. I put the kettle on and lied in detail about my marriage.

When I'd finished reeling off all the nonsense I'd prepared with Jez, she said, "Your life's probably quite dull, isn't it?" and traced a well-manicured finger over my palm.

"Horribly predictable," I concurred.

"That's so hot!" She kicked off her shoes and rubbed her feet against my legs.

"You just fall into a routine," I continued. "Sharing the ironing, writing shopping lists, updating the direct debits on the joint account."

"Say that again!" Meena rubbed her toes against my groin. "Please!"

I had only got as far as *shopping lists* when she straddled my kneecap and started rocking backwards and forwards.

"Now," she panted. "Tell me what you did this weekend and make it boring."

"I took the in-laws to a garden centre."

Her breathing accelerated audibly.

"Borrowed a spirit level off the bloke next-door."

She began to gasp.

"And erected a bookcase."

We made love for a few seconds at a time in six different positions and she climaxed in time with the kettle.

"You're new to this, aren't you?" Meena asked, on her way out.

"I'm a virgin ...at adultery."

"Good. Pleasure deflowering you. There's nothing more desirable than someone else's faithful husband." She winked and shut the door behind her.

Now, don't get me wrong, this didn't work every time, but it did work a lot more often than I had expected.

Debbie was a rather melodramatic Mancunian who sang all her songs as if she were performing a death scene at the opera.

At the end of her third lesson, we got talking and I told her I was married. She said I looked like I needed cheering up.

I agreed that I did.

She nibbled my neck. "You don't taste married."

I kissed her. "Nor do you."

"I should. My husband betrayed us both by marrying me when he didn't mean it. I might be unfaithful, but he's faithless."

"Sorry. I didn't realise you were married too."

"Don't add guilt into the mix," she said. "I like my adultery unadulterated."

"When would you like it?"

"Thursday."

My imaginary marriage was going through a honeymoon period – sex on tap, no strings, no drama. But everything changed when I met Alicia. She was an adorable Afro-American with a Gospel voice so powerful, it filled the street, as she danced, clapped, and whooped her way through my songs.

I worked with her intensely, getting her to whisper the words, close her eyes and give an intimate delivery. I had never taught this well before. The effect was incredible. Musically, she couldn't have been more responsive, but nothing else happened.

One day, I decided to teach her my new song. Her rendition was fragile, honest, and entrancing. My song had found its natural singer.

I decided to move in for the kill. "I'm married, you know."

She congratulated me politely.

I explained that it wasn't really anything to be congratulated about, as my wife didn't understand me.

Alicia gave me a hug. I punched the air, inwardly.

"I'm really pleased you told me that." She let me go and looked straight into my eyes. Alicia really was one of the most beautiful women I had ever seen in my life. I couldn't believe my luck, until she said, "I can help. I'm a marriage guidance counsellor."

"Oh God...good." I felt like fainting.

"I've got plenty of time," she said, kindly. "Tell me all about it. Please."

We sat on the sofa while I improvised about my non-existent marriage. "It's a question of irreconcilable similarities," I lied. "We're totally compatible – it's a nightmare. We've got the same taste in music, we've travelled to the same places, read the same books – we've got nothing new to tell each other. I know what she's about to say before she says it and it's the same for her, so we've stopped talking – there's no point."

She reached into her jacket and offered me a handkerchief. I took it and dabbed away imaginary tears.

Alicia asked me tactfully about my sex life. I told her that my wife and I had rampant sleep seven times a week and this morning I had made mad, passionate love to my wrist.

She listened sympathetically. "It's all about communication."

"We have an unspoken understanding – we're not speaking."

"Communication is like dancing."

"Is it?" She had a highly encirclable waist, so I couldn't help saying, "Show me."

She did. It wasn't as good as a date, but I enjoyed myself. I told her she had some great moves. She said I danced, "Like prose in motion". I asked her out to a salsa club, but she advised against me ever dancing in public.

We laughed about my sense of rhythm until it was time for her to go. On the way out, she said, "You and your wife just need quality time together. We'll talk about it at the next counselling session."

"You mean, the next singing lesson."

"Of course. My mistake. Now, spend some time with your wife."

I was in love, but that didn't stop me dating my other clients. Kerry the Kiwi took me to a one-man performance of *Finnegan's Wake* and back at her place we shared a soggy expanse of cold, Ethiopian flatbread and vegan dips. She detailed her PhD on "The build-up of volcanic activity over geological timescales," then took all night to orgasm. Afterwards, she said "That was the fastest climax I've had in years. I can't believe your wife lets you out of the bedroom."

"My wife?" I scoffed. "She just crosses her legs and thinks of Iceland."

Thursday came around and it was time to date Debbie the melodramatic Mancunian. Beforehand, she explained that we would have to be careful because her husband had married her for money and if we ever got caught, she would lose half her anti-surveillance business.

After Debbie had outlined her security protocols and exit strategies, I complained that the date was turning into a spy film, but she just said, "I thought you fancied a bit of undercover activity.".

We arrived at the hotel separately and signed in under aliases. She frisked the room for bugs, then I frisked her for fun. I snogged her for a bit, but she broke away and whispered, "Stop! Footsteps!" and put a finger to my lips. After what seemed like a decade, she withdrew her digit and said, "It's okay, you can carry on now."

We snogged for another few seconds before she broke off again with a "Wait! I'm sure I heard a key turn." After another lengthy hiatus, she said, "Must have imagined it. Carry on."

A little later, Debbie climaxed in characteristically operatic style, bursting into tears of joy. At this, someone knocked on the wall. I couldn't really blame them, but it was the end of the world for Debbie. "I've broken our cover! Hide!" She threw herself under the bed and dragged me down with her.

After we had lain on the carpet for several minutes, she handed me a card. "Here's my address."

"Doesn't your husband live there too?"

"It's a dead letterbox."

There was a knock at the door. That really did it for Debbie.

"We'll have to evacuate!" Debbie raced for the fire door. I tried to follow, but she turned and held her hand to my chest. "We can't risk being seen using the same fire escape."

"There's only one."

"Don't worry." Debbie pointed at the window. "The place is covered in scaffolding."

I climbed out.

"I'll make sure you're not followed," Debbie said as she locked the window behind me.

I found myself outside the ninth floor of the hotel stood on what I had thought was scaffolding but was in fact a window-cleaning platform. This came as a bit of a shock and, in my initial panic, I dislodged a bucket and watched it drop onto the road one-hundred-and-fifty feet below. As it impacted, I was so overwhelmed by vertigo that my legs gave way, and I passed out on the platform.

I woke up on the pavement several hours later. I must have been winched down by the window cleaners. One of them had plonked a mop on my head.

I wasn't at my best, but I made sure I arrived home in time for Alicia's lesson.

"You look upset," she observed.

"It's nothing," I replied.

"I can tell," she said. "I'm trained."

It was awkward. I couldn't tell her about my window-cleaning trauma, so I looked out of the window for inspiration, and said, "My wife's been having an affair."

"You poor thing." Alicia hugged me.

"I've only just found out," I said.

This didn't accelerate the comforting process in the way I'd wished. She just said, "Don't blame her. It's the fault of the marriage. You just need to understand why it happened."

"Things hadn't been right for a while," I admitted with as much regret as I could muster.

"I know this must be painful for you," she said. "But you need to rebuild trust."

"I can't look at her. I don't have anything to say."

"Arguments are like onions."

"Tear-jerking?"

"Layered."

"Oh."

"Let's try a role play," she suggested.

This was more like it. "Shall we dress up?"

"No," Alicia replied. "Just imagine I'm your wife and you are having a calm, honest conversation."

I took a moment to manoeuvre my mind into a place where I could role play my made-up marriage.

"You ready?"

"Yes."

"Okay, let's begin." Alicia straightened her stance and her expression.

What would I say to my unfaithful wife if she existed? I opted for route one: "Was he better in bed than me?"

Alicia, gently annoyed, broke out of character. "Don't demand intimate details of the affair. You'll only hurt yourself."

"Okay. Sorry." I looked at Alicia, sat there all gorgeous and attentive, and I heard myself say, "Why don't we have sex?" before I remembered it was meant to be a role play and added, "... anymore?"

Alicia remained focused on her role. "I've been under a lot of stress at work recently."

"I know, dear."

"Let's try to find more time for each other," she continued. "Take more interest in each other's lives and feelings and try to sort out our sexual problems."

"Agreed."

"Let's commit to a new future together."

I liked the sound of that so much, I tried to kiss her.

She wasn't interested, but luckily, she just laughed it off.

Life became a carnival of dodgy dates. Manic Meena took me on an oxygen bar crawl. After I'd got her going by cataloguing my imaginary wife's tedious hobbies, we had sex on the London Eye. Kerry the

Kiwi took me to an epic poetry evening in a community centre and she proposed a threesome with me and my wife, but after I told her that my wife was too much of a prude, we made do with a twosome. Melodramatic Debbie insisted we met at a goth bonk-bar, claiming that the black leather bondage outfits provided ideal cover. We had a heart-to-heart and she told me how romantic it was to meet someone else who understood what it meant to be unhappily married. After we'd retired to a dungeon-themed shag-room, she quipped, "If you're mad enough to believe in marriage, you deserve to be committed for life to an institution."

I almost lost count of the wife-related porkies I told along the way:

She laughs like a Kalashnikov, snores like a blue whale and farts like a Harley.

The sex is athletic but meaningless – I need it to mean more.

She never goes out. Her idea of an evening on the town is walking the recycling bin up the path.

It was cruel, but given that she didn't exist, I wasn't slandering anyone.

My next lesson with Alicia was exquisite. She performed my new song like an angel, finding nuances that I had never imagined. Afterwards, I praised her to the skies and laid into my wife so much, it backfired.

"You're spouting industrial quantities of nonsense," Alicia protested. "You're lying to yourself. You've no self-esteem and you don't value your partner. Maybe that's why your marriage is shipwrecked. You need a win-win style of arguing. Share a walk in the park, a drink in the pub or a coffee in the shops – value each other. Accept your life stage."

"Is *washed-up* a life stage?" I enquired.

"You're only washed up if you admit defeat," she replied.

"That's so true. Will you go out with me?

"I don't date married men."

"What if I left her?"

She laughed briefly, realised I was serious, then burst into tears. It turned out that she cared

I thought it was probably time to ditch the imaginary wife. The question was, how? I decided to visit Jez. It was the middle of the night, but that was usually the best time to catch him in.

Jez's house was never hard to find. His entire terrace vibrated to the sound of drumming. I noticed that most neighbouring buildings were subsiding and had been covered in supportive scaffolding. I leant on the buzzer. There was no response, so I climbed through the open window and fell awkwardly onto his floor.

If Jez had thought I was a burglar, I would have been dead. Instead, he just looked down on me, said "Thanks for dropping in," and played one of those rimshot and cymbal crash combos once popular in cabaret clubs.

"Jez, this is serious."

"Looks like you've had a humour bypass."

"I have. And no one was around to give me an anaesthetic. My life's a mess. I wish I'd never invented a wife."

"Look, mate." Jez wheeled himself closer. "What else did you expect asking a drummer for advice?"

I laughed, he laughed, and not for the first time, we decided to exchange drummer jokes:

"What do you call a drummer with half a brain?"

"Gifted."

"How can you tell if the stage is level?"

"The drummer drools from both sides of his mouth."

"What do you call a drummer who splits up from his girlfriend?"

"Homeless."

There were no jokes about vocal coaches, but that didn't stop me thinking that my entire life was nothing more than as a joke.

"What's the best way to finish all these affairs?" I asked Jez.

"Tell them she's dying, pregnant or suspicious," he replied.

"Who?"

"The imaginary wife, of course." Jez wheeled back behind his kit and resumed his drumming.

He didn't have to say any more. I left via the window and fell headfirst into a bin.

Over the next fortnight, I ended my affair with Meena by telling her that my wife had died and my affair with Kerry by telling her that my wife was pregnant. There were tears and insults, but what else did I expect?

I feared that dumping Debbie would prove more complex, particularly as I was going to have to do it at the School Disco-themed evening she'd insisted we attend as cover.

On the fateful evening, I stood in a draughty hall looking a prize plonker in my cap, tie, and shorts. Debbie arrived a little late, carrying off her pencil skirt and ponytail with panache.

"Feeling nostalgic?" I asked.

"Takes me right back behind the bike shed." She pinched my bum.

I took her hand. "It's been amazing."

"It *is* amazing," she corrected.

"It was," I said.

"Was?"

"Sorry about the tense."

"I like tense," Debbie said. "It's calm I don't do."

"I can't go on like this," I said. "The guilt, the subterfuge..."

"Yes, isn't it great?"

"Breaking up is hard to do," I said.

Debbie saw that I was serious and went nuclear. "A failed mistress! I can't make my marriage work and I can't break yours up. I can't even make a go of my affair!" She burst into tears.

I heard sobbing from across the room. Another adult schoolgirl was also in tears. It was Alicia.

I strode over, trying to intercept her approach. "What are you doing here?"

"I wanted to catch a glimpse of the wife whose marriage I'd persuaded you to end," Alicia said.

"How did you know I was here?" I asked.

"Never mind that," Alicia said. "I've got to say something. I feel terrible."

Before I knew it, Alicia was speaking to Debbie. "You must be..."

"The other woman." Debbie said, bitterly.

"But that's me," Alicia replied.

"No," Debbie said. "You're the wife."

"That's you," Alicia said.

"Is it?" Debbie asked.

I weighed in with a "Sorry."

"Who are you apologising to?" they enquired in unison.

"Both of you," I said. "And my wife. All three of you, in fact. Oh, listen to that. The DJ's playing Madness." I skank-danced to the ska, but they didn't join in, so I decided that my only option was to come clean. "I've been lying to you both. I don't really have a wife."

Debbie howled with anger, hit me, and left.

Alicia just said, "I like comedians, but I don't want to date one. You wrote such an emotional song, but you have no emotion in your life – just games. I love you just the way you aren't."

"I've lost you, haven't I?"

"You never had me."

After sulking solo to *Don't You Want Me Baby?* I left the disco, pulled off my wedding ring, and booted it into the wasteland.

When I got home, Donna was in the kitchen with a pair of *Screaming Orgasms*. For a minute, I thought I was hallucinating; it had been months since the break-up.

"I'm so sorry," she said. "The tour gave me time to think, and I've realised what I need. I want someone monogamous and dependable like you. Will you give me another chance?"

I had no imaginary wife and no real girlfriends, so I caved in.

Later that evening, I told her all about my new song, and she tried it out while I accompanied her on the piano.

Her performance had none of the fragility of Alicia's rendition, but it was still beautiful. My drawing danced before my eyes: Elvis Presley, the one-legged angel, and the crazy golf course. It was magical.

When she had reached the end, Donna hugged me. "You're a genius! Leaving you was the biggest mistake of my life. I want to rebuild our relationship."

We lived together for many happy weeks before she stole my song and left me for the boss of a record label. My song is on her solo album, *Sensitive Resentment*, along with her hits, *Brittle Anger*, *Bishop, I Defy You* and *So Cross with Your Cross*. I decided to give up song-drawing and women. Now, I just play at weddings.

***

I placed a consoling hand on the pianist's shoulder. "Can you play your song?"

"I can do an instrumental."

"I hate instrumentals."

He gave me a wicked grin and belted out a song with exquisite piano accompaniment and a voice so grotesque it sounded like a vixen birthing triplets. Sometimes, sound is better seen and not heard.

As I endured his caterwauling, I thought about my eight failed marriages and wondered why any man would want to invent a wife. If I kept going at my current pace, I would soon have enough real ex-wives to field a football team. What would I call them? Vindictive United, perhaps.

Relationships are all about delusion. We fall in love with our own idea of someone else and we're surprised when they don't live up to it. Why do we do this to ourselves? Wouldn't it just be easier to watch pornography? Once the song was over, I decided to head home and do exactly that.

RULE 10 - WORK HARD, DIE HARD

I once met a man who had survived a daytime television show about Christmas decorations. It was a twenty-eight-part series for The Living Room Channel, and there was more than one fatality.

I had just broken up with my fifth wife and she had marked the occasion by emptying a pint of bitter over my head. I managed to get the worst of it off with a bar towel and, even back then, I didn't have enough hair to ruin.

Still, I wasn't at my happiest, so I scanned the room for a potential drinking partner. Most people were coupled up, or in groups. There was only one other loner, and he was hard to miss. The bloke wore an Argentina football shirt with Diego Maradona's name on the back. It was the kind of fashion choice that could get an Englishmen hospitalized, had he not been north of six-foot-six.

I've always liked contrarians, so I made a lame quip about the deceased South American footballing cheat and joined him for a lager. After we had shared moans about the government, social media, and the weather, we got talking about the worst jobs we'd ever had. I told him how I had once trained as an acupuncturist and hit an artery, and in return he revealed his involvement in the doomed festive filming. He was quick to point out that although he had been the boom operator, he was not personally responsible for the catastrophic *boom* that had obliterated the director, the producer, and the location. I had the feeling this wasn't the first time he had made play with his boom pun, but I humoured him with a chuckle, eager to learn more about the tinsel-themed tragedy.

"It all kicked off in the London Borough of Ealing," he began in a deep deadpan. "We were in a detached house in a leafy crescent. Outside, it was a blazing day at the dog-end of August. Inside, it was Christmas. The lounge was stuffed with seven or eight Norwegian spruces, bauble mountains, colossal brandy bottle towers and mince pie pyramids. There was a coal-effect gas fire, and, on the table, trays of sloppily iced biscuits had been hacked into the shape of abominable snow men. What with all the camera lights and the heatwave, it was a bit like celebrating Christmas on an Australian beach, except indoors.

The producer was married to the director and neither of them seemed particularly happy about it. I could see why - she was an embittered bitch with status issues, and he was a surrendered husband choking back resentment at a lifetime's humiliation. The cameraman was a storied Scot on the brink of retirement, the researcher was so pregnant she looked ready to drop, the runner had all the wisdom and experience of a new-born chimp, and the lady presenter looked ready to book a place in the nearest nursing home. The A-Team this wasn't.

The producer appraised the excessively merry decorations and asked the room, "Do you think it's Christmassy enough?"

I knew better than to reply, so I just continued reading a book about timecode. It had some interesting ideas about synchronization systems and outside broadcast operations.

"I don't want it to look bare." The producer lit a cigarette. This was the early noughties and people did that sort of thing all the time, but it didn't help the researcher, who coughed violently and clutched her baby-belly.

The director said, "Maybe another bauble," and sunk his teeth into some Nicorette gum.

The researcher struggled to her feet, added a bauble, and stepped back to check her work, triggering a bauble avalanche.

"Listen!" The producer wielded her cigarette like a weapon. "We've got twenty-eight half-hour programmes to record this week. There's no time for mistakes!"

The researcher looked up gloomily from the festive mess and said, "Sorry."

"Don't you apologise, honey." The producer gave the researcher a patronizing smile. "It was my husband's fault."

"Sorry, dearest." The director sounded like a man accustomed to apologizing.

While the producer nursed her cigarette, everyone else gathered up the escaped baubles. I wanted to appear willing whilst making the least effort possible, so I reached down and examined a single bauble with great care, raising it to my ear and shaking it. I've never been convinced that all baubles are entirely hollow, and this was a golden opportunity to listen to whatever was hidden inside.

While I conducted my experiment, the cameraman crawled around the carpet gathering armfuls of the shiny spheres, and muttering Glaswegian obscenities. The researcher did her best to help but scrabbling around on the floor hurt her back and made her breathless. The runner used a bauble to examine his reflection and adjust his hair. The director used his feet to shuffle baubles rather morosely into a shiny heap.

Once everyone had finished, the presenter tripped backwards onto the gathered pile, crushing most of the baubles to shards.

"Look! "The producer's nostrils flared as she shrieked. "*Christmas Present* is the first series Nepotism Productions have made for The Living Room Channel! If we're going to build on the success of *Tiling Tips* for Planet Bathroom and *Dog's Dinners* for The Canine Channel, we're all going to have to..." She paused for emphasis. "... *concentrate*!"

"Absolutely, dearest." The director grimaced. "Shall we go for a take?

"Nay bother, pal." The cameraman jumped into action. He clearly couldn't wait to get it over with.

Sharing that sentiment, I snapped, "Phones off!" It was an important instruction and part of my job, but I also enjoy shouting at rooms.

The cameraman switched on the remaining lights. Most of them were fitted with festive red gels. A tacky image of Santa and a sleigh was projected onto the curtains.

The runner switched on a dilapidated camcorder popular with twentieth century wedding guests. Noticing this for the first time, the director mumbled, "Christ, dearest."

The producer seemed unperturbed. "What?"

"Where did that contraption come from?" the director asked.

"My dad's attic," the producer replied. "I thought a second camera might speed things up."

"But just look at the monitors!" The director indicated two video screens. "Jim's got a decent camera. It makes the world seem a colourful, pleasant place to spend a lifetime. But young Ben here has a very different kind of camera. It makes the world appear grey, hazy, and mystifying. They'll never match."

"You're going to have to make them," the producer said.

"How?" the director asked.

"Make Ben's camera look less grey, hazy and mystifying," the producer said.

"I can't," the director replied. "It's cheap and decrepit. That's the best it can manage."

"Then make the good camera look cheaper," the producer said.

"Nay bother, doll." The cameraman adjusted a dial. "That hazy enough for you?"

The producer looked thoughtfully at the monitors. "Maybe a little more out of focus,"

"Right you are, boss. How about that?" The cameraman turned the dial again. "Mystified yet?"

Both monitors showed equally blurry images of the festive decorations.

It would have been pointless proceeding had the producer not taken a moment to look daggers at her husband, allowing the cameraman to correct the focus on his camera unobserved.

Noticing this, the director gestured for the presenter to step into place and said, "Let's turnover."

"Wait for the plane to pass!" I interrupted. There weren't any planes, but I like to keep myself amused. I watched everyone stand in unnecessary silence for twenty seconds. The researcher closed her eyes and rubbed her back, the runner yawned, the cameraman looked at his watch. The producer glared impatiently at the director, who shrugged.

I stared intently at the ceiling as if observing the imaginary aircraft through the plaster. Once I'd got bored, I announced that the plane had passed, and the crew lumbered back into action.

"Running up." The cameraman looked through his eyepiece. "Speed."

"And action." The director cued the superannuated presenter with a chopping motion, somewhere between an orchestra conductor's sweep and a weak Kung Fu move.

"Hello, and welcome to Christmas Present," the presenter began. "Your up-to-the-minute guide to festive fare, gorgeous gifts, and yummy yuletide surprises. I'll be here for the next twenty-eight days with tip-top tips on how to make your Christmas go with a bang."

A bulb exploded. The researcher screamed. The presenter swooned, decking a Norwegian spruce, and carpeting the mince pies.

"Christ!" the producer shouted.

"God!" the director added.

"Brandy!" the presenter implored.

"There you go." The researcher passed her a bottle from a decorative tower.

"Thank you, dear." The presenter took a glug. "When are you due?"

"Not for another three months," the researcher replied. "It feels like forever."

"I know dear, but it'll be worth the wait. My grandchildren took decades to arrive."

The cameraman was removing the blown bulb and searching for a replacement when the producer interrupted. "Anything serious?"

"We'll live," Jim the cameraman replied. "It's only a bulb."

"Then get it fixed!" she shrilled.

"Nay bother, doll." Jim knew how to humour a deluded paymistress, however imperious her manner. But that didn't mean he didn't want to kill her with his bare hands.

The runner approached the director, like a puppy seeking a scruff. "Am I doing all right?"

"Magnificently." The director yawned.

The runner beamed gormlessly.

The cameraman finished inserting the new bulb and turned to the director. "There you go, pal. Do you want us to do that again?"

"Yes," the director replied.

"No," the producer said. "We can get the scissors in before the explosion."

"Fantastic." The director spoke like a man who knew that the editor's metaphorical *scissors* couldn't. He turned to the presenter. "How are you feeling?"

"A little shaky, dear." She swigged more brandy from the bottle. "But I'll soon be right as rain."

"Are you sure?" the director asked.

"Oh yes, dear." The presenter took another glug.

"Well, if you're absolutely certain," the director said. "Let's go for a take."

I seized my moment in the limelight with a "Phones off!"

"They already are!" the producer protested.

"Just checking," I lied.

"So," the director consulted his script. "Snow beasts."

"*Edible* snow beasts." The producer emphasised the word *edible* as if her husband's life depended upon it.

I could almost smell her overbearing anxiety as she approached the presenter. "Remember, you mention them here, but you don't actually make them yet. The edible snow beasts are the *part one climax*."

"Okay dear." The presenter took another swig of brandy.

The researcher waited for her to swallow it before handing over a tray containing paper, scissors, glue, a jar of viscous liquid and an empty milk bottle.

Once the director satisfied himself that everything was as ready as it was ever going to get, he attempted a cheery, workaday smile. "Shall we turnover?"

"Nay bother, pal." The cameraman's reply was almost instantaneous. He really did seem desperate to get it all over with, and looking around the room, that general sentiment prevailed.

That being the case, this seemed like the perfect opportunity to wind everyone up again. I cleared my throat and shouted, "Wait for the plane to pass!"

Everyone stood in frustrated silence. The producer lit another cigarette, the director masticated more Nicorette gum, the cameraman stared gloomily at his watch, the presenter swigged more brandy from the bottle, the researcher shut her eyes, and the runner yawned so widely that his jaw locked, and he had to whack his chin with the heel of his hand to close his mouth.

At that, I decided to put them out of their misery. "Okay. It's gone now."

The producer sighed. Everyone assumed their positions.

Jim manned his eyepiece. "Running up... Speed."

The director's Nicorette gum had practically glued his teeth together, but he managed to squeeze out an "Action!"

"Today," the presenter chirped into the lens, "We're going to make edible snow beasts and flammable biscuit bushes, but first a snowman snowscape in an inverted milk bottle." She cut out a paper snowman, glued it to the inside of a milk bottle and poured in the gloopy liquid. The snowman flopped soggily against the glass and began to dissolve.

The director watched this on the monitors. The blurrier of the two pictures started to rock.

"I'm sorry," the runner said, his hands shaking uncontrollably on the camcorder. "But that's the crappiest thing I've ever seen in my life."

I failed to contain myself, as did the cameraman, and director.

The producer was furious. "How dare you?"

Everyone apologized insincerely. Apart from me. I couldn't be bothered.

The producer turned to the presenter. "Why are you apologising?"

"It was my snowman who flopped. I should have made him waterproof. I'm afraid I just didn't think it through."

"Don't worry, honey. You're doing just fine." The producer turned to the director. "Would you like to have a quiet word?"

"Not particularly."

"I said, come here and have a word."

The unhappy couple retreated to a corner, imagining that their conversation was private. They were wrong. I'd dropped a live radio mic into the director's arse pocket, and I monitored their conversation through my headphones.

"She's lost it!" The producer panicked, in an under-the-breath shout. "Bloody hopeless, totally senile and probably pissed."

I heard the director swallow his gum in a pained gulp.

The cameraman stood his equipment down, conscientiously disconnecting leads, removing the matte box and replacing the lens cap.

The runner struggled to mimic this procedure with his considerably less impressive kit. "Having fun?" the runner asked, attempting to bond.

"Aye, very merry," the cameraman replied. "I love listening to that nippy producer cow bumping her gums and I'm absolutely over the effing moon about you filming the entire frigging series out of focus. She might as well have hired her granny to shoot it."

"Her granny's doing the website," the runner said.

"Good for her," the cameraman said.

"How's your hotel?" the runner asked.

"The shower seeps slime, there's nay toilet in the toilet and I'm the only guest not seeking asylum."

"Getting any kip?"

"Aye, when they're not wailing to Albanian folk music, they're shouting about blood feuds or trying to flog me dead flowers. It's about as peaceful as an Old Firm Cup Final in the marching season."

That seemed to bring the conversation between the runner and the cameraman to a close, so I switched my attention to the other side of the room. The researcher was standing beside the forest of Norwegian spruces, showing a copy of her scan to the presenter.

"He's got a lovely big head," the presenter cooed, cradling the brandy bottle.

"Thanks," the researcher replied. "But that's his bum. His head's down there."

"Well, that's lovely too, dear."

"Edible snow beasts next," the researcher said.

The presenter handed the scan back. "Have you got my bits dear?"

The researcher put away the scan and fetched a tray containing pastry, icing sugar, raisins, greaseproof paper, a metal dish, assorted plastic shapes and some complete edible snow beasts.

"Thank you, dear," the presenter said, and took another swig.

The producer returned from her supposedly confidential contretemps with the director, and said, "Right, let's not waste any more time."

"Nay bother, doll," the cameraman said.

The director summoned what little remained of his professional enthusiasm. "Shall we change the set up?"

"We haven't got time," the producer said.

"Okay," the director said, sounding far from okay. "Let's go for a take."

"Nay bother, pal." The cameraman switched on the lights.

The director turned his attention to the monitors. "Turnover."

I hesitated for just long enough to offer them hope, before saying, "Wait for the plane to pass." Was I being childish? Yes. Did I enjoy it? Yes.

Everyone stood in silence, waiting for the passing of my imaginary aircraft. The researcher shut her eyes, the presenter swigged brandy, Jim consulted his watch, the runner failed to stifle a yawn, the director cradled his chins. The producer glared at me with such intensity that I felt obliged to pretend to follow the plane's trajectory through the ceiling with my boom pole. Rarely has a piece of sound kit moved more slowly. Eventually, once I had given the imaginary plane enough time to cross most of the Atlantic, I said, "Okay. It's gone."

"Running up," the cameraman said as he fiddled with his equipment. "Speed."

"And action!" The director cued the presenter.

"Children love abominable snowmen," the presenter began, "And sometimes they're good enough to eat, especially if they're made of pastry and covered in icing sugar. Here's how to make edible snow beasts."

"Hang on!" the producer interrupted. "I've got an idea.

"Christ!" The director shouted, before adding a "dearest."

"What?" The producer looked as belligerent as a cage fighter.

"It's just that it was going well," the director replied. "What's your idea?"

"Let's use the fire!" the producer exclaimed with the enthusiasm of a visionary prophet. "What could be more Christmassy than a real fire?"

"But it's not real," the researcher said.

"We know it's not real." The producer winked. "But the viewers won't."

"It's a coal-effect gas fire," the director said.

"Precisely!" The producer raised her hands for emphasis. "It's an effect. A special effect."

"Brilliant!" The runner seized the chance to suck up. "Like an explosion!"

"Exactly. That's the spirit." The producer inhaled a lungful of smoke. "At Nepotism, we pride ourselves on our ambition. Turn on the fire." She exhaled.

Once the researcher had finished coughing, she gave the fireplace a dubious look. "Do I really have to? It looks a bit dodgy to me."

"So does my husband," the producer laughed. "But I still turn him on."

"Now, now dearest." The director cringed. "Don't embarrass me."

The researcher shook her head in disgust, turned on the gas tap, and asked, "Can someone give me a light?"

"Here." The producer dangled her cigarette in the researcher's face. "Use this."

"Thanks." The researcher took it and attempted to light the gas tap.

The producer looked down at the researcher's bulging belly and summoned a shade of humanity to her tone. "What are you going to call it?"

"If it's a boy, we might call it Jack. If it's a girl, then maybe Daisy."

"Daisy? Jack?" The producer spat, instantly transformed back into harridan-mode. "Children are wasted on your generation. You name your daughters after cows, your sons after peasants and you stay at home so you can't afford proper childcare."

"I won't need childcare," the researcher said.

"Nor will I!" The producer's face crumpled into tears.

I hadn't expected that. Until now, the producer had shown all the emotional fragility of a frozen halibut. I watched her retreat to the corner with the director and listened in to their conversation once again:

"Just one more cycle might do it." The producer sounded oddly childlike.

"That's not what the doctor said, dearest," the director replied.

"Bloody IVF! Sounds like a terrorist group."

"Well, it's terrorised us for long enough. We've done all we can, but even if Nepotism goes global, we can't buy the impossible."

"Without kids," the producer sniffed. "There's not much future for Nepotism."

I didn't want to hear the producer sobbing, so I removed my headphones.

Regrettably, the runner took this as an invitation to talk to me. "You know there used to be a TV show where you win everything advertised in the commercial break?"

I offered him a blank expression.

"Well, if the Living Room Channel did it, you'd win a stair lift, life insurance and debt counselling." The runner exploded with boundless mirth.

It was probably an accurate observation, but I didn't want to encourage him to continue talking to me.

I looked across the room. The researcher was still struggling to light the gas tap with the producer's cigarette. The presenter was stood beside her, drunk and maudlin.

"No one's really interested in my edible snow beasts, are they?" the presenter asked.

"I am," the researcher replied. "And don't worry, so are they." She pointed at the camera lenses.

The producer caught the end of this, and weighed in. "Are they?

A few misguided souls in nursing homes and mental hospitals might have you on in the background, but don't delude yourself - no one is sad enough to listen to what you say and least of all to make an edible snow beast!"

The presenter burst into tears and left the room. The researcher stamped out the cigarette and ran after her.

I couldn't help reflecting that these developments didn't bode well for Nepotism and the twenty-eight festive episodes yet to be recorded, so I consoled myself by listening in to the producer's "private" conversation with the director in the far corner:

"Was that necessary?" the director asked.

"Yes!" The producer replied.

"Bang goes the series!" the director said.

"Who cares?" The producer was losing whatever grip she'd ever had. "As ideas go, it had about as much going for it as *The James Cordon Hotpants Workout*.

"That idea had legs," the director replied.

The producer hit him with the edible snow beast tray and lit up another cigarette.

I was feeling hungry, so I stole a mince pie from the set and gobbled it whilst watching the cameraman pack away his kit.

"Well," Jim sighed, as he capped his lens. "That just about takes the kipper's knickers." He has always had a poetic turn of phrase. You get that with Glaswegians, along with the violence.

The runner's kit had about three parts, so didn't take long to put away. As he zipped up his single case, he asked, "Can anyone else smell gas?"

"No, laddie," the cameraman replied. "Just a load of hot air and that's odourless."

"Is it?" The researcher said on her way back in from consoling the presenter. "Around here, I think it smells of Nicotine!"

The producer squared up to her, armed with her latest cigarette. "How dare you?"

The researcher wasn't backing down. "How dare you break an old lady's heart and choke my unborn child with your filthy smoke all day?"

"She might be enjoying it for all you know," the producer replied.

"What makes you think it's a *she*?" the researcher asked.

"Because you seem like a sensible girl." The producer smiled thinly. "Where's our presenter?"

"She's gone to see her grandchildren," the researcher replied.

"Well, off you bugger too," the producer said. "Go on, drop your sprog."

"Fine." The researcher turned to go.

"What are you doing spawning at your age anyway?"

"I'm nearly thirty."

"That's nothing."

"It's all relative, I suppose."

"What do you mean by that?"

"Well, to a teenager, twenty-nine is just this side of ancient."

"And?"

"You're the other side of ancient."

"You're not fit to be a mum!" The producer shrieked.

The director apologised to the researcher and led the producer to their corner. They were both still completely unaware that I could hear their every word through my headphones:

"Leave her alone, dearest."

"But she's pregnant, for God's sake!"

"I know, but don't blame her. Her biological clock was ticking. It's not her fault if yours has stopped. It's a very nice clock. Good enough for my mantelpiece, but the mechanism is beyond the repair of ... the finest watchmaker in Switzerland."

The collapsing marriage went silent, so I removed my headphones, looked back into the centre of the room, and saw the researcher offer the runner a lift.

The runner hesitated and turned to the cameraman. "Am I still needed?"

"Are any of us?" Jim had already packed up most of his camera gear.

The producer removed any remaining doubt by storming back into the centre of the festivities and shouting, "Get lost the lot of you and have yourselves a merry bloody Christmas!"

The director raised his hands to the ceiling like a surrendering soldier. "Thank you, everyone."

A few minutes later, I was out in the summer sun with Jim, loading our gear into the back of the crew van.

The shoot hadn't been filled with an excess of jolly incidents, so anecdotes were in short supply, but Jim did eventually turn to me and say, "We're nowhere near a flight path, are we?"

I thought about lying but couldn't be arsed, so I shook my head.

"There never were any planes?"

"No."

"Oh."

Jim's a decent bloke, so I felt he was due an explanation: "I don't like Christmas."

"I suppose it's all right in December." Jim unscrewed a lens. "What is it now?"

"Fourth of July."

Jim grinned. "Happy Independence Day!"

An electronic crackle reminded me that I'd forgotten to retrieve the director's unnoticed arse-mic. Having just escaped the house, I didn't relish rushing back inside, so I decided to eavesdrop on the couple one last time. I put my headphones on and listened in:

"We're never going to have any kids, are we?" the producer said.

"No, love," the director replied.

"That's right. No love."

"We've still got each other."

"And?"

"Our work."

"What, edible snow beasts?"

"Don't be silly, dearest."

I heard the crunchy sound of violence being exacted on festive biscuits.

"There's one thing we can still share," the director said. "Give us a fag."

"They're the one thing we have that's not disposable."

I heard the flick of a cigarette lighter, followed by a gas explosion. The coal-effect fire had finally been lit.

***

I offered to buy the boom operator a pint to thank him for his story, but he explained that he had to be up early to film a corporate video for an arms dealer. It was well-paid and he was keen to give it his full attention.

RULE 11 - THE LAW HAS LONG ARMS AND HAIRY LEGS

I once met a police inspector who had narrowly escaped being rendered into a block of lard. It happened during an investigation into a series of poltergeist-related incidents and the experience had turned every hair on his head snow white.

We met over a pie. I was dithering between steak-and-kidney and gammon-and-cider, and the inspector offered some unsolicited advice. He was a man who knew his pastry inside out, and, once he had persuaded me to follow his example and opt for the gammon, I suggested he join me at my table. He explained that his name was Inspector Wildgoose, and he was recovering from the strangest case of his career.

I asked him if he would mind giving me the lowdown and he was kind enough to oblige:

***

"It all began when I was assigned the poshest partner on the planet. She was a flame-haired sergeant named Herring and she seemed more suited to a pony club than Salisbury nick. Her favourite expressions were "Golly Gosh!", "My Sainted Aunt!" and "Cripes!", and I wondered whether she had ticked a diversity box for "gormless numpty".

The Super clearly despised her and made a point of sending us on fool's errands to get Herring out of his hair. This time, we'd been dispatched to the village of Wiggle-under-Bullock to interview a local lunatic about his paranormal delusions.

On the plus side, we had a shiny new patrol car. For years, I had been chuntering about in a clapped-out old banger well below the dignity of my pay grade. Now that I finally had a decent motor, I would have been failing in my duty if I hadn't put the sirens on full blast and hit one-hundred-and-twenty for a solid hour. The sirens not only alerted other motorists to my rapid approach, but they also blocked out Sergeant Herring's drivel about "county balls", "gorgeous hunks", and "show jumping".

When we passed through a dense forest, I dropped down to ninety-eight. My caution was rewarded when I narrowly dodged a rutting buck. The last thing I wanted was to prang my new motor on a hundred kilos of fresh venison.

Wiggle-under-Bullock looked to have all the standard-issue attributes: duck pond, pub, church, vicarage, farm, and cottages, but it also boasted multi-coloured bunting advertising the annual *Lard Festival*. A hunch told me it might be a tad less thrilling than Glastonbury.

The moment I parked outside the complainant's condemned barn, a scream issued from inside. Herring shrieked in sympathy, which wasn't helpful.

I kicked a door, which disintegrated on impact, and we walked in on piles of elaborate agricultural contraptions. A wild-eyed scarecrow I took to be the complainant was running a lathe along a miniature guillotine, the source of the screaming sound.

"Don't worry, officers," he explained in an accent nurtured over generations of inbreeding, "It's a badger trap. Completely humane. Decapitation is almost instant."

"Yuck!" Herring exclaimed, like a weening infant.

I had encountered more savoury individuals than the complainant, but I decided to keep things polite. "Good morning, sir. What seems to be the problem?"

"Cursed!" he declaimed, like a demented prophet. "The whole village is cursed! Ever since the committee drowned Mad Ethel."

"Gosh!" Herring exclaimed.

I swallowed a "bollocks". Had the superintendent's fool's errand turned into a murder investigation? "What committee drowned whom?"

"The committee drowned Mad Ethel in the duck pond, of course." The complainant's expression suggested that I had to be a moron for not knowing this. "She was accused of witchcraft, wasn't she, but proved her innocence by drowning."

"And when was this?"

"1592."

Herring's brow furrowed. "Ninety-two minutes past three?"

"No," the complainant replied, impatiently, "1592."

"The sixteenth century?" I'd heard of cold cases, but this was pushing it. Why on Earth had we been sent here? The Super really knew how to waste police time.

I turned to go, but the complainant wasn't having it. "I'd like to report my poltergeist for breaking and entering. I've had frogspawn in the washing up, sticklebacks in the shower and pondweed in the bath. Last night, I heard the squish of soggy footsteps in the attic and a bloodcurdling quack."

"A bloodcurdling quack?" I queried.

"Undead ducks," he explained.

I retreated for a quiet word with Herring. "You know why we're really here, don't you?"

"Haven't the foggiest," she replied.

"Could you try irritating the Super less?"

"I don't see what that's got to do with it."

"You don't, do you."

"No."

Herring really didn't, so I decided to spell things out for her. "I'm stuck out here in the capital of nowhere when I could be back at the station catching up on paperwork and it's all because you should be on *Downton Abbey* rather than on the beat."

Herring looked close to tears.

I adopted a more conciliatory tone. "Surely, you'd noticed. It's not the first time the Super's sent us on a wild goose chase, is it?"

"A wild goose chase for ...Inspector Wildgoose!" She giggled uncontrollably and knocked over a cardboard box. It fell apart on the floor, releasing a cloud of gunpowder.

"Mind your step, officers," the complainant warned belatedly. "That's my pyrotechnical area. I'm working on ways of exploding foxes. It's a quicker death than hunting."

"Golly," Herring said with a soppy smile. "How thoughtful of you."

I'd had enough. This bloke didn't need the cops, he needed a good seeing to from the RSPCA. "Does anyone else live here? A social worker? A wife, even?".

He looked subdued. "The wife's passed. Cancer of the arse. Terminal."

I apologised. Herring sobbed. The complainant lent her a handkerchief, but it was covered in badger blood.

We made our excuses and left. I couldn't wait to hit the road again. The trouble was the road was empty. My first new patrol car in twenty-two years was nowhere to be seen. I despaired. "Tell me it's not true!"

"That would be lying, sir," Herring replied.

The complainant shouted after us, "I told you this village was cursed!"

We were going to have to investigate the theft of our own patrol car. It was a colossal embarrassment, but in all my years as a copper, I had never been more fired up about a case.

We could discount the complainant, as he had been busy telling us about his badger guillotine, undead ducks, and fox explosives at the time. It had to be a local – outsiders had no reason to pass through a place with no discernible attractions.

The nearest building appeared to be a vicarage. The clergy didn't tend to specialise in grand theft auto, but they might know their parishioners. It was a start.

The vicarage's heavy oak door was answered by a tweedy woman clutching a handful of piano keys. "How can I help you?"

"We've had our car stolen," I said.

"Have you informed the police?" she asked.

"We are the police," I replied.

She invited us into a spacious living room dominated by a grand piano. It was a magnificent specimen, but every key was missing.

"Looks like a rather unusual accident," I observed.

"The piano tuner got a bit carried away." It was not a convincing reply.

"We've been speaking to your neighbour," I began. "The gentleman with a grudge against wildlife."

"He has a few too many bats in his belfry, poor chap," the woman replied. "But don't underestimate him, he's made a bomb."

"Jolly wealthy, is he?" Herring asked, as a colossal explosion rang out across the village.

"No," the woman said. "He's made an actual bomb. That was probably it, I should think."

"Golly," Herring observed.

I looked out of the window. The soot-faced complainant gave me a thumbs-up from the remains of his barn. There appeared to be no human casualties, so I continued my dogged pursuit of our patrol vehicle. "We've heard mention of a curse. Do many cars disappear?"

"Like planes in the Bermuda Triangle, you mean?" she asked.

I nodded, trying not to mentally replay the Barry Manilow ditty.

"Never," the woman said. "It's always been a peaceful village."

"Are you the vicar?" Herring asked.

"Don't be silly," the woman replied, whilst applying some glue to the base of a piano key. "We're not a bunch of lefties here."

"Understood. I don't suppose we could borrow your car for an hour or so," I asked. "Just so we can look for ours."

"I'm afraid not," the woman replied, as she placed the glued key into the grand piano's toothless gob. "But if you toddle over to St Judas's, my husband might be able to help."

Even though I resented the word *toddle*, I thanked her and wished her the best of luck rebuilding her piano.

St Judas's church was a gothic monstrosity decorated with some of the grimmest gargoyles I had ever clapped eyes on; every one a stone-faced insult from the mind of a maniac. The interior was even worse - grisly depictions of blokes being martyred inventively and an aisle rug depicting Mad Ethel's terminal ducking. Expert knitters had captured her turmoil and the surrounding villagers' cruelty in exquisite detail.

I am not one to jump to conclusions, but the current vicar was a supercilious bastard.

"So, the first time the constabulary deign to pay a visit to our community," he sneered, "it's because they've had their panda stolen."

I wasn't having this. "We actually came here because your neighbour complained about some rather distressing occurrences."

"I wonder who that could have been," the vicar replied with unholy sarcasm. "Did these distressing occurrences involve undead ducks, by any chance?"

"Well guessed!" Herring trilled, clapping her hands in glee. It was like being partnered by a girl guide.

The vicar stared at her in disbelief for a cold ten seconds. "Let me look in the Sunday school storeroom. I'm sure we can find you both something suitable." He sloped off down an annex and returned with two small bicycles. They had been designed for pre-pubescent girls and were covered in stickers celebrating princesses and ponies.

Herring seemed delighted with her bike, but I can't say I was.

The vicar gave me an evil grin. "I'd start with Midwinter Farm if I were you. They manage most of the land around here, so your vehicle is as likely to have been torched on their patch as anywhere."

"You really are too kind," Herring said.

Kind would not have been my word of preference, but at least the vicar offered us directions. "They're just along Hangman's Lane. Take the third left after The Crow Road and Midwinter Farm is at the top of Drawquarter Passage."

"Thanks." It didn't sound like a particularly scenic route.

"If you reach Armageddon Avenue," he added, "you'll have gone too far."

We wheeled our way down the aisle, mounted our bikes in the graveyard and cycled past the village green. My bike was designed for a child under five-foot tall and, as I pedalled, my knees were almost level with my chin.

"If you don't mind me saying sir," Herring said, "You do look particularly foolish on your pink pony bike."

"Thank you, Herring."

"I suppose it should help you lose a little belly fat." Herring was not big on tact.

I sulked all the way to Midwinter Farm. Two signs welcomed visitors: *Well-Endowed Bull For Hire* and *Wanted – Old Tarmac*. A rustic bloke watched our arrival with incredulity. I didn't blame him: we weren't just strangers, we were a pair of plonkers on pink, princessy pedals.

"And who might you be?" The farmer gave our wheels a scornful look. "The soppiest chapter of the Hell's Angels?"

"What a wonderful farm!" Herring exclaimed. "You must be very proud."

"I pinch myself regular," the farmer deadpanned.

"We're here to investigate the theft of a car," I showed him my badge.

"And whose car might that be?" he asked.

"Ours," I replied.

"He's nicked your car, has he?" the farmer asked.

"Who's he?" I asked.

"The local crime wave," the farmer said.

"I wouldn't want to jump to any conclusions," I said.

"Jump away," he said. "No other bugger did it."

"Who is the local crime wave?" I asked.

"The village teenager," the farmer replied.

"Is that an official position?" I asked.

The farmer bristled. "Don't you try your big-city sarcasm with me."

"None intended," I lied. "Where can we find him?"

"In your car I should think," the farmer said, unhelpfully.

"Got a bit of a track record, has he?" I ventured.

"Too right he has. Yesterday morning, the little bugger pelted me with free range eggs and the other week he showered the missus with bull semen."

"Bull semen?" Herring furrowed her brow. "Where on earth did he get that from?"

"Bulls," the farmer explained.

"Yuck!" Herring ejaculated.

"Look," the farmer said, wearily. "When you find him. Hand him over to the village committee and we'll string the little bastard up, pelt him with stones and bury him in the woods."

"If it's all very well, I'll keep it a police matter," I replied. "Village committees can't order lynchings."

"We used to," the farmer said.

"This is the twenty-first century, sir. Not the sixteenth."

"Standards have slipped. I don't like to whinge, but I'm a farmer and it comes naturally."

"Understood, sir. But that doesn't help us retrieve our police car, does it?"

"Where did you have it last?"

"We parked it outside the badger-killer's barn," I replied. "Before his bomb exploded."

"And what were you doing there? Listening to a load of slurry about Mad Ethel I shouldn't wonder. You don't want to believe old

Jethro."

A woman approached with a basket. We showed her our badges, but she only had eyes for our princess bikes. Once she had stopped laughing, she tilted the basket towards us. "Try one of these. Goose eggs. Give you the runs, but they're a real food. Fancy one?"

"No thanks," I replied. It wasn't a difficult decision.

"Are you related?"

"Nothing wrong with incest!" She bristled.

"I mean, are you married?"

"For my sins, yes." She smiled at her husband.

He didn't smile back. He just said, "And mine."

"Tell us about the village teenager," I said.

"Poor lad is very troubled," the farmer's wife said. "Who wouldn't be after what happened to his parents?"

"And what was that?" I asked.

"It's a gruesome story," the farmer's wife said.

"Oh gracious," Herring said. "I think I'm about to get the collywobbles."

"Well, for most of the year," the farmer's wife said, "his parents were a popular couple, but the trouble always came at Christmas. Although they were both tone death and laryngitic, they insisted on going carol singing. People would tell them they were dreadful, but they wouldn't listen. Every year they'd go door-to-door murdering the spirit of Christmas. Their caterwauling would turn the milk sour, distress the chickens, and make the sheep howl. The village committee even made a formal complaint, but that didn't stop them. Then, one year, just after they had reached "I saw three ships come sailing by", a combine harvester careered down Black Dog Hill and harvested them alive."

Herring screamed. "Golly, how ghastly."

"It made the committee's litter-pick a little tricky. We wanted to win the *Best Kept Village Contest*, you see, and we'd have stood no chance with diced body parts scattered all over the green. Mikey took it all to heart, poor lad."

A double combine harvester-shredding would not have gone unnoticed at national level, let alone at the local nick. But the deaths were not my immediate priority. I wanted my car back. "Where does young Mikey live now?"

"With his aunt, Anna," the woman replied. "But the less said about her the better. She's one of the village red-light districts."

"You have more than one?" It seemed that Amsterdam had nothing on Wiggle-under-Bullock.

"There's one red-light district at number thirty-six, and another red-light district at number forty-seven," the farmer replied.

"Golly!" Herring exclaimed, jiggling on the spot. "I've always wanted to visit a real-life red-light district!"

My sergeant truly was a prize specimen, and we all took a while to stare at her appreciatively.

After a bit, I thought it best to move the enquiry along. "Where might we find this woman's red-light district?"

"Up Trotter's Bottom," the farmer replied. "Along Cousinkiss Way, take a left into Deliverance Lane and it's at the top of Rider's Mound. Can't miss it."

I thanked the rustic couple, and we cycled off through a succession of muddy lanes to a ramshackle street of unnumbered cottages. After we had pedalled up and down for a bit, we found one with a red lightbulb in the porch. It seemed a safe bet, and this was confirmed when my knock was answered by a woman in a leopardskin negligee.

"We're looking for the red-light district," Herring blurted out, excitedly.

"Good for you," the woman replied.

"Is this it?" Herring asked.

"Depends who's asking," the woman said.

"The police," I replied, flashing my badge.

"Then you've come to the wrong place." She rearranged her attitude. "This is strictly legitimate."

I looked at the array of hardcore erotic equipment in the hallway. "How exactly?"

"I'm an osteopath," the woman explained. "An intimate osteopath."

"Super!" Herring said. "Can you do my back?"

"I specialise in fronts," the woman elaborated. "Male fronts."

I could feel the woman's eyes on my crotch, so I said, "The farm sent us here."

"It's nice to be recommended," she scoffed. "And what exactly are you looking for?"

"The village teenager," I said. "Mikey."

"It's taken you rozzers long enough to take an interest in our village," the woman said. "Why start now?"

"He may have stolen our car," I said, ruefully.

"Oh, I see. It's only when you get your own car nicked that you bother to show up. Anyway, I'm the wrong frontal osteopath. You're looking for Anna."

We said our goodbyes and cycled up and down for a bit longer. Eventually, Herring squealed and pointed at a red lightbulb dangling in the porch of a near-identical cottage further up the road. We knocked at the door. There was no answer.

As I stood beside my ridiculous sergeant and our princess bikes, I couldn't help reflecting that I had been involved in more successful operations. So far, we had interviewed a deluded lunatic about some undead ducks, lost our patrol car, met a woman with a keyless piano, borrowed a pair of girls' bikes off the snarky vicar, paid a fruitless visit to a farm and met an unhelpful prostitute posing as a "frontal osteopath".

"I'm jolly hungry," Herring blurted. "I could eat an entire herd of cattle."

For once, I had to agree with Herring.

We cycled back to the village centre. *The Witch and Duck Pond* had a sign depicting a submerged crone surrounded by diving mallards. It didn't promise fine dining and luxury, but when it came to pubs, Wiggle-under-Bullock offered a choice of one, so we left our bikes by a window and went in. A real fire raged between a skittles alley and a bar billiards area, and there was a pile of village newsletters headlined, *Ghost Worries Sheep*.

A young woman of South-East Asian appearance stood boredly behind a counter offering *Classic Wiltshire Ales and Local Thai Food*. I gave her a smile and asked for the menu. She dipped below the bar and re-emerged clutching a card reading, *I Don't Speak English*.

I tried talking slowly. "Can I speak to the landlord?"

She dipped below the bar again and returned with another card reading, *Back In 5 Mins*.

I thanked her for very little and flicked through the village newsletter. Features included *Bait That Badger*, a report from a poaching convention and a lengthy preview of the Lard Festival. Last year's winner was the vicar's wife, and she was pictured holding a pristine tray of exquisitely rendered fatty tissue. There were many photos of previous contests: inter-war lard, sixties lard, millennium lard. Most villages were content with cake-bakes and novelty vegetables, but clearly Wiggle-under-Bullock was no ordinary village.

After about twenty minutes, a formidably ugly bloke walked in, looking deeply displeased to see customers. "No food after two," he muttered in a local grumble.

When I pointed out that it was ten to one, he handed me a menu in untranslated Thai. It wasn't helpful.

"What do you recommend?" I asked.

"All depends on what you like, don't it?" the landlord asked, impatiently.

"Fish and chips?" Herring ventured.

"Do me a favour," he replied.

"Pie?" I suggested.

"Wrong continent."

"Thai pie?" Herring guessed.

"Enough of this," he said. "You'll have two specials and that's an end to it."

We looked through the open kitchen door as the woman prepared the mysterious meal with great violence, throwing knives at vegetables, pummelling ingredients, and massacring meat with machetes. A flame surged, then there was a furious burst of flash-frying and rigorous plate-plonking.

The landlord brought us the specials, reversed a chair, and sat astride it like Christine Keeler as he watched us eat. "You're not from these parts, are you?"

"No, sir," I replied through a mouthful of mystery-meat. "We're not."

"Then what the hell are you doing here?" he asked.

"We're on police business..." I began.

"It wasn't my combine harvester," he interrupted.

The landlord's defensive panic would have raised my suspicions were I investigating the double murder of the tone-deaf carol singers, but that was not my main concern. "We're investigating a car theft."

"And whose car might that be?" he asked.

"Ours," I said.

"What makes you think it's in my village?" he said.

"We parked it here," I replied.

"That was careless," he said.

"Was it?" I asked.

"Looks like it," he said.

There wasn't anything special about the special – just some spicy noodles and gristle.

I felt like complaining, but before I could, Herring blurted out, "Absolutely yummy! My compliments to the chef!"

The landlord just stared at us until we had finished, then said, "Fifty pounds eighty."

I thought the meal was worth about a quid, but I had my police credit card with me.

"Cash only," the landlord said. "Service not included."

I emptied my wallet and requested a receipt. He claimed his printer was broken. I said that a handwritten one would do, provided it was on headed paper. He scrawled something illegible on the corner of a village newsletter and tore it off. I trousered it and headed for the doors.

Herring skipped after me. "Cheer up, sir. Why not turn that frown upside down?" Her sympathy was as welcome as a dose of syphilis, but she didn't notice this. "Shall we take the scenic route? If we go through the woods, we can loop around to the red-light district in no time."

I had no interest in scenery, but it would at least enable us to scope out the vicinity for my car. We remounted the princess bikes and set off.

I must admit, the woods were idyllic – unspoiled stretches of oak, ash, and redwood. I was almost starting to enjoy the ride when a giant bloodhound sprang out of a hollow and charged at us. Herring veered off into the trees. I hit the brakes and nose-dived over the handlebars. The next thing I saw was a grizzled bloke looming over me, holding a shotgun to my head, and snarling the word, "Poachers!"

"Police officers," I gasped, prising my badge out of my pocket.

"Stone me, the rest of the country gets The Flying Squad, and we get The Barbie Bunch." The man waved his shotgun about in disgust. "You cyclists are just like ramblers - too bloody mean to pay for petrol."

"Where's my sergeant?"

"Under my dog."

I looked further down the lane and, sure enough, Herring lay beneath the bloodhound, whimpering.

"Can she get out?" I asked.

"Not unless Fang lets her," he replied.

"Call him off, please. We need to get to the red-light district. It's urgent."

After a long pause, the man shouted, "Fang! Mercy! No Kill Today!"

Fang released Herring, who crossed herself and repeated the word "Golly" on a loop.

I struggled to my feet and watched the man hook up my princess bike with his shotgun barrel.

"So," the man said, "You urgently need the red-light district?"

"Yes," I replied. "The second one."

"Right you are. You go down Coffin Lid Lane and along Gallows Way as far as Cutthroat Cottage. Then it's thirteen yards up Butcher's Alley, just before Vulture's Close. You can't miss it."

I thanked him, nursed my injuries, and did my best to console Herring.

"Now off you bugger." The man strode off with his hound.

Herring's cycling was now noticeably more erratic, but she soldiered on to the second red-light district. When we got there, all was not well. The woman who worked as the first red-light district was having a screaming match with a woman who looked as if she worked as the second red-light district. I may have been making the kind of assumptions that would get a Tweeter cancelled, but I am a detective inspector, and she was wearing thigh-high leather boots, a suede mini-skirt and a breastless t-shirt.

"I told you!" the first woman shrieked. "I'm the only red-light district in this village!"

"You lying whore!" The other woman shouted. "The red-light district is here at number forty-seven! It's been in my family for generations."

I couldn't let this escalate, so I thrust out my badge. "Look, can't you both work peacefully alongside each other?"

"Why?" the second woman asked. "Fancy a threesome?"

I did, but there's a time and place for everything and I was more concerned about my stolen patrol car.

No doubt influenced by my arrival; the row climaxed prematurely. "I'll get you, Anna," the first woman threatened, as she strutted off. "This village is too small for the pair of us."

"Call yourself a red-light district? You're no more than a knocking shop!" The second woman walked into her red-light district. When we followed her in, she turned angrily and snarled, "Ever heard of knocking?"

"Sorry. We forgot this was a knocking shop." Herring burst into floods of giggles.

Sometimes, I despair of junior officers.

Noting my disapproval, Herring said, "Sorry, sir. I thought that was the sort of joke men of your age liked."

It was, but I was not about to let her know that. The cottage was uncannily like the first red-light district, with copious erotic accoutrements arranged at cheeky angles. Herring couldn't suppress her giggles at the eye-opening array of dildos, but we weren't here to admire penile-substitutes we were here to get our new patrol car back. I didn't waste any more time.

"Are you the mother of the village teenager?"

"What of it?"

"There's a rumour he might have stolen our car."

"Got any proof?"

Before I could reply, Herring chipped in with a "No."

It wasn't helpful, so I tried distracting the woman with another question. "Do you have a picture of Mikey?"

"Of course. What kind of mother do you take me for?" The woman walked over to a whipping bench, unlocked a compartment, and took out a framed photo of her sharing a spliff with a teenage boy in a blue-and-amber football shirt.

"Shrewsbury Town!" Herring blurted, like a University Challenge contestant on a starter-for-ten.

"Well, aren't you clever," the woman said.

"I never took you for a football fan, Herring," I said.

"Loads of gorgeous hunks!" Herring exclaimed.

"Town are only in the third tier," the woman said. She took a chocolate finger out of a box and sucked its end off. "I can name a second suspect."

Finally, a breakthrough! I looked at her expectantly.

"Mad Ethel." Her words dashed my optimism in three syllables.

Herring wasn't slow to find the theory's fatal flaw. "Isn't she a ghost?"

"She may be dead," the woman said. "But don't hold that against her. She's as alive as you or me. Terrible hauntings, she gives. Only the other night, pints were pouring themselves in the pub, the piano was playing itself in the vicarage and the tractor was possessed."

"The tractor was possessed?" I stifled a chuckle.

"That's right," she said. "Possessed. Driving itself in circles it was. And howling."

"Howling?" I queried.

"Carburettor like a banshee. Made my blood run cold."

"And the piano?" I asked.

"Played itself. There was an invisible plonker."

"In the vicarage!" Herring exclaimed, as if this connection between the keyless piano and the spooky nonsense required a Poirot to spot.

"Right," I sighed. "On the off-chance that Mad Ethel didn't take our car, where can we find your son?"

"No idea," she replied. "But I can tell you where to find Mad Ethel."

"The graveyard?" I ventured.

"Her bones, perhaps. But her spirit dwells in the duck pond."

"Jolly good." I was running out of patience, and ready to resort to sarcasm. "I'll get on the phone to the police diving unit right away."

As we hit the princess bikes and cycled back to the village centre, Herring seemed far from her usual cheerful self.

"Golly, sir, ghosts can be extraordinarily scary, can't they?"

"You're a police sergeant, Herring, not a girl guide. Pull yourself together and think of the force."

"I can't help it, sir. I was drummed out of the girl guides for desertion."

I was about to challenge the veracity of this claim when I caught sight of something so incredible, I almost fell off my princess bike: the outline of our patrol car.

"It's here!" I shouted. "I can see it!" My heart skipped. Finally! This was shaping up to be one of the happiest moments of my life.

It was not until I had reached the village green that I realised the appalling truth. My beautiful car was being dragged backwards from the duckpond by an elderly tractor. I had waited five years for a new vehicle, and within twelve hours it was swimming with the mallards.

"The pond's probably chock full of clues!" Herring gushed. "Should we be thinking about donning wetsuits and flippers?"

"No," I replied, fighting back tears. I could barely speak.

"I'm just trying to think outside the box," Herring protested.

"Well," I said. "If you're not careful, you'll end up thinking inside a box. A dark wooden one." Harsh, I know, but I wasn't in the best of moods.

We released our bike stabilizers, and watched the tragedy unfold. I thought of my new car's rear axle steering, virtual exterior mirrors, and super-cruise control and wept. For me, this was akin to witnessing the death of a prize bull at the hands of a toreador: a calamity of legendary proportions. I was lost in grief, right up until the moment I saw the skeleton at the wheel. It was wearing a Shrewsbury Town shirt.

The farmer leant out the tractor window and took great pleasure in saying, "Found your car for you, Inspector."

"Thanks," I replied. "But don't touch anything. The car's a crime scene."

"It's a write-off," the farmer said. "And so's the village teenager."

"Herring," I said. "Would you call Forensics?"

"For the body, sir?"

"For both," I replied. I turned to the farmer. "We'll need to cover the vehicle before we get a proper pathology tent in place."

"We've got a marquee," he offered. "For the Lard Festival."

I thanked him, prematurely. The marquee turned out to be a

multi-coloured monstrosity illustrated with an array of clowns and circus animals; bunting, balloons and inflatable pigs dangled from the top.

I didn't feel festive, I felt bereft: the loss of a new car can unman a man. Once we had enlisted some villagers to erect the tent, we went inside to take a closer look. It was a heartless crime, killing off the car – what kind of person could bring themselves to drive such a masterpiece of modern engineering into a duckpond, and cut it off in its prime?

Herring seemed more concerned with the driver, which struck me as incredibly cold. I was a colleague and I had just lost my car.

"It looks ancient," Herring observed.

"Time of death?" I asked.

"Probably Tudor," Herring replied.

"So, a Tudor stole our car this morning."

"They were lawless times back then."

"This morning?"

"The sixteenth century."

I was in a state of mourning for the vehicle, but that didn't stop me from getting irritated by Herring. I could have given her a good talking to, but it wouldn't have made any difference, so I decided we'd be far better off doing some actual detective work.

"Let's ask some awkward questions," I said.

"But won't that be a bit embarrassing, sir?" Herring objected.

"For the culprit, yes."

"But for me too, sir. Socially, I'm highly sensitive."

"You're a police sergeant, Herring. Pull yourself together."

I swallowed a "snowflake" on my way out of the makeshift pathology marquee and stopped to interrogate the farmer, who was still milling about the duck pond. "Where were you earlier today?"

"I suppose I was mostly farming," he replied.

"Really?"

"I was up a cow. You wouldn't believe how roomy they are. I got both arms in."

"Who found the car?" Herring asked. It wasn't a bad question, but the sound of the word *car* made my heart sob.

"It was the gamekeeper," the farmer replied. "He reckons his hound can smell death underwater."

"I suppose we'd better pay him a visit, then," I said.

"He's not hard to find if you know where you're going." The farmer speed-blurted some mindboggling directions and re-mounted his tractor.

Forty minutes later, we had abandoned our princess bikes and were stumbling through thick undergrowth.

"I'm sure he said it was the fifty-third oak on the right," I said. "How many do you make it so far?"

"Two-hundred-and-twenty-four. This is rather like orienteering. I remember at Roedean - AAAAAAAARRRRGH!"

The ground opened up beneath us and we fell twelve feet into a mantrap.

For the second time that day, the gamekeeper looked down at me. This time, though, he knew we weren't poachers.

"I suppose you'll have come about the death then," he said, before helping us haul ourselves out of the mantrap.

He took us to his cottage, which would have been a hospitable gesture were it not for the overpowering stench. The air was thick with dog hairs, animal heads were mounted on every wall, and the sound of his hound supping water from the toilet bowl with its enormous tongue made thought difficult. "Make yourselves at home," he said.

Herring looked admiringly at a particularly grotesque example of cervine taxidermy. "Nice Bambi."

"I stuffed him myself," the gamekeeper replied. "He was a troublemaker, didn't fit into the herd, so I slaughtered him. I know he was young. Still an adolescent really, his whole life ahead of him and I cut it short. Just one carefully placed bullet and Fang did the rest."

The hound ran up and pinned me to my chair. The gamekeeper seemed unconcerned and walked calmly out of the room.

"Please don't go away," I pleaded from under the dog.

The gamekeeper returned with a slab of raw meat. Fang bounded off me and devoured it noisily.

"Don't you mind Fang," the gamekeeper said. "Underneath all that blood-encrusted fur and solid muscle beats a heart of gold."

"Wonderful beast," I said, after I had regained my ability to breathe. "How did you find the car?"

"Very easily," he replied. "It was the only one in the duck pond."

"Can you explain your whereabouts over the last twelve hours or so?" I asked.

"I've been mostly stalking and culling, but the only witnesses were deer, and I killed every last one of them."

"Do you enjoy murder?" Herring enquired, with a naivety that only I knew was genuine.

"I love animals," the gamekeeper replied. "But they're generally better off dead. I strangled most of these myself." He indicated the mounted heads. "Jethro uses machines and explosives, but I think bombs are for cowards. You know where you are with brute force."

We thanked the gamekeeper and returned to the crime scene. The clown-covered marquee was doubling as both a pathology tent and a lard festival venue. There may have been a skeletal Shrewsbury Town fan inside the corpse of my defunct patrol car, but that hadn't stopped the villagers from assembling a jolly array of rosettes, bunting and stalls.

The farmer's wife approached with a tray of lard. "Hello, Inspector, I hope you don't mind me asking, but do you like my rendering?"

I hadn't got time to assess her fat, so I just said, "It's terrific."

"I'm a little worried about the texture," she persisted.

"It looks very smooth to me," I lied without looking.

"We're going to need a judge for the lard contest, Inspector, and you seem to have a good eye."

"I'm in the middle of a case, so, I'm a little tied up."

"Go on, Inspector, it'll only take a few minutes. I'm sure we'd all be extremely grateful, a big cheese like you judging our lard." She giggled.

A three-fingered hand grabbed my elbow. It was Jethro, the animal exploder whose poltergeist issues had dragged us out to Wiggle-under-Bullock in the first place, and he was desperate to show me his lard. "What do you reckon to my consistency, Inspector?"

"You're consistently barking, I'll give you that."

He just stood there, looking crestfallen.

Herring joined us. "This is all rather jolly, isn't it?"

I looked at the drowned patrol car and its long-dead driver and begged to differ.

"Where were you earlier today?" I asked Jethro.

"When exactly?" he replied.

"All of it," I said.

"I suppose I was mostly inventing ways of killing animals."

"Did anybody see you?"

"You, the guillotines, the explosives, the bombs."

If ever there was a candidate for Rural Psychopath of the Week, I was looking at him. "Thank you, sir," I said. "You've been extremely helpful."

I led Herring out of the marquee. "Any news from Forensics?"

"Oh, they're not coming," she replied.

"Not coming?!"

"They didn't think we were serious."

"But someone drowned my car and a Shrewsbury Town-supporting skeleton."

"They thought it was a prank, sir."

"Did they remember doing an autopsy on a pair of carol singers diced by a combine harvester?"

"No, sir. More of a jigsaw than an autopsy, I'd have thought. They were sure someone at the morgue would have mentioned it, as they always enjoy discussing gruesome deaths in the canteen."

There was an otherworldly sound from across the pond. Dusk had fallen and it didn't make the village appear any more wholesome.

"Gosh!" Herring shivered. "Bit creepy round here, isn't it?"

"Creepy as buggery, it is," a familiar voice added. Jethro had followed us out, and I wished he hadn't. "We've got all the usual suspects here," he continued. "Legless boggarts, headless horsemen, screeching brownies."

Herring grinned. "I used to be in the Brownies."

"Brownies!" Jethro exclaimed. "Brownies will chew your flesh off and make your skull scream for all eternity."

"Some of them were quite wild," Herring replied. "Our pack in particular."

There was another gruesome noise. Herring froze in her tracks.

"That'll be Charlie's bull fitting," Jethro explained. "Big William's epileptic, see."

"Shouldn't someone call a vet?" I asked.

But Jethro was off on one. "It's a cursed region, this. You've got The Wild Witch of Wookey, The Creech Hill Bullbeggar, and the dreaded double-headed dragon of Shervage Wood."

"Oh no!" Herring was aghast. "That many ghoulies!".

"I've only just started," Jethro continued. "There's a headless highwayman who holds up a zombie stagecoach every third Tuesday. There's an invisible vulture that crosses the skies searching for lost souls at teatime. There's a demon hill-giant with a pair of monk's heads where its eyes should be, and don't forget the whistling spectre who hangs out in an abandoned burial barrow near Devil's Den."

I was about to tell Jethro to shut up when I noticed that the duck pond was bubbling.

"It's the mallards weeping for their spectral mistress," Jethro explained.

"Golly," Herring said.

"One day," Jethro said, "When Mad Ethel's put to rest, we'll hear the silence of the ducks."

I could turn a blind eye to the skeletal Shrewsbury Town fan and the combine harvester cold case, but I couldn't let the car theft go. It was getting late, and, other than the borrowed princess bikes, we had no means of transport. We were going to have to set up base.

Holiday Inns were not exactly abounding, so I asked Jethro, "Do people ever stay in the pub?"

"Stay in the pub? I'd rather pickle my left buttock in formaldehyde."

It was an enduring image, which was unfortunate. I'm not sure why I had sought advice from a lunatic.

Herring and I walked into *The Witch and Duck Pond*. It was hosting a one-a-side quiz between the farmer and the gamekeeper:

"Who played the villain in *The Wicker Man*?" the landlord asked.

"Idris Elba," the gamekeeper growled.

"Roger Moore," the farmer said.

After the first six rounds had ended nil-nil, I ordered a pint of bitter and a large Pimm's for Herring.

"There you go, Inspector." The landlord passed me the drinks. "A poncy great Pimm's and a pint of *Pigmelters*, brewed specially for the lard festival. I hear you're the judge."

"Vicar's wife told you that, did she?" I wished I hadn't been railroaded into agreeing. "Any chance of a couple of rooms?"

"Haunted or exorcised?" he replied.

"Exorcised please," Herring said, hurriedly.

"That was just my little joke," the landlord said, mirthlessly.

Herring laughed excessively.

"Full Thai breakfast?" the landlord enquired.

"Sure," I replied, without thinking.

"One hundred and eighty-seven pounds each," the landlord said. "Cash in advance."

I always carry plenty of cash to bribe informers, but this pretty much cleared me out.

The landlord explained that there was only one room in the pub, but there was nothing indecent about it, as it had a bunk bed. His wife showed us along creaking corridors to a door with a felt-tip notice reading, *Do Not Attempt to Repair Anything*

Herring bagged the top bunk and asked, "Have you got an umbrella, sir?

"No.

"It's just that, if Mad Ethel shows up, I might wet myself and I am inclined to urinate copiously at times of stress."

After we had swapped bunks, I suggested sleep. But rather than obey her superior officer, Herring chose to jabber on: "This village gives me the willies. Do you think it's twinned with Mordor?"

"Quite possibly. Good night, Sergeant Herring."

I didn't sleep well. Howling, screaming, and assorted otherworldly sounds filled the night. I just dismissed this as general rural racket, but the thought of our lost patrol car kept me awake. After Herring's eighth whimper, I agreed to go downstairs and investigate the empty pub. The fruit machine was emptying itself, spirits were escaping from the optics, and *Ghostbusters* played on the juke box. I can't say I was scared, but I can say that a moment later, I was unconscious.

I woke up staring at a two-dimensional clown. The red, blue, and yellow slapstick-purveyor had been sewn into the inside of the marquee roof and was looking directly at me. I tried getting up, but I was tied to something as cold and hard as a mortuary slab. My skull throbbed, but I managed to turn my head sufficiently to see that the entire village had assembled. It was just like a fair, but instead of a brass band they had a human sacrifice. Me.

The vicar climbed onto the roof of my drowned car and addressed the gathering. "Welcome to the Lard Festival. I know you've all been busy melting your fattest hogs and whether you've used kettle rendering, dry rendering, or steam jackets, let's hope that the results are smooth, creamy and of a non-rancid, buttery consistency."

There was an enthusiastic round of applause, then a rendering machine was wheeled into position above my head. It blocked out my view of the roof-clown, but that was a smaller concern than the cluster of rotating blades descending upon my body.

I tried to remain calm but failed. "I should probably shout for help, shouldn't I?"

"If you like," the vicar replied.

"HEEEEELLLP!"

"Feel better now?"

"Not particularly."

"I'm sorry to hear that," the vicar said. "I'd so like the last few minutes of your life to be as comfortable as possible."

"So, that will be why you've dangled rendering equipment over my head."

"No. That will be to turn you into lard."

"How many people have you turned to lard?"

"A few dozen, I dare say," the vicar conceded. "I don't mind admitting that some outsiders have a certain subhuman charm, but most of them are better off as lard."

The vicar's laughter mingled with the rendering blades in my mangled mind. This was the opposite of dying peacefully in bed. I looked at the marquee ceiling's clowns, bunting and balloons - my final sight on Earth. What a way to go.

My despair was interrupted by a collective gasp from the villagers. Had they suddenly rediscovered their humanity? No, they were gasping at the sudden arrival of Mikey the village teenager. He was aiming his mobile phone like a ray-gun, recording my impending rendering. It didn't seem much of a weapon, but he shouted like it was a stick-up: "This is a live stream! You've been rendering outsiders for years! My mum and dad weren't having it, so you shredded them with a combine! Now, it's all over TikTok!" He noticed the skeleton seated in my former patrol car. "And you've even nicked my Shrewsbury Town t-shirt and stuck it on Mad Ethel! You bastards!"

The farmer ran at Mikey, who swerved out the way, sending him crashing into the marquee's central supporting pole. Clown-covered canvas enveloped us all and halted the rendering machine's progress.

Eventually, female hands freed me from the canvas with a "Golly, sir!" Herring gawped at my sacrificial stone, and asked, "Are you quite alright?"

"Never been better, sergeant."

"It's just... your hair."

"Never mind my hair, just untie me."

Herring obliged with her pocket-knife and, before long, I was free, albeit looking like Gandalf The White.

Although Forensics and the Super would have been happy to ignore our pleas for assistance, they had to respond to a TikTok controversy, and the village was soon aflush with pandas.

The entire population were arrested, accused of both mass murder and food safety violations. Mikey, the village crime wave, was the only innocent party – he explained that he had been strung up in the forest by the village committee in preparation for The Lard Festival's closing ceremony: a celebratory stoning. He had managed to escape by swinging relentlessly until a branch broke, and he'd been able to get away in time to film the incriminating festive footage. Herring had failed to detect any signs of my impending sacrifice by staying in her bunk bed and had only come down to check on her Full Thai Breakfast.

***

The inspector's story was over, and our pies were a distant memory, but at least dessert was on the horizon. While the barman fetched the menus, I took the opportunity to clear up a few details.

"How did your car end up in the duckpond?"

"Village-wide conspiracy. They wanted to render me, so the bastards took our means of escape."

"How about the Shrewsbury Town-supporting skeleton?"

"A bit of intrigue to perplex us and keep us in town until I'd been rendered."

"Bit like The Wicker Man?"

"But with lard."

"And Mad Ethel was real?"

"Possibly. A place like Wiggle-under-Bullock had been the centre of so much killing over the years, it's no surprise it attracted the odd poltergeist."

"Why didn't they try to render Herring?"

"More lard on me, I suppose, what with my lifelong devotion to pies."

The barman gave us the dessert menu. It offered the prospect of cheesecake, jam roly-poly, spotted dick and Eton mess, but we both went for the lardy cake. When it arrived, it didn't taste of human at all, I'm pleased to say.

As I chewed my way through the lardy cake, I thought about events at Wiggle-under-Bullock. People like to bang on about community spirit, and the village had both a community and a spirit. It would have been better off with neither, as the community only existed to render strangers into lard, ostracise teenagers, and duck witches to death; and the spirit broke pianos, possessed tractors, and wasted perfectly good alcohol.

Was country life just about red-light districts, poltergeists, and murder? Or did England's green and pleasant lands have more to offer? What about hunting, shooting and incest?

Cities have their drawbacks too, with their gangs, their traffic, and their surfeit of humans. So, what's the alternative? The suburbs? Semi-rural, semi-urban and full of semis, they may seem like the ideal hybrid. But I don't do safe and anonymous – I far prefer dodgy and characterful, as my extensive selection of ex-wives attests.

At the end of the day, you're better off enjoying your own company and ignoring your neighbours. That way, it doesn't matter where you live, and there's no one to grass you up.

RULE 12 - SPIRITUALISM IS BEST KEPT IN BOTTLES

If my intimate dealings with the human herd have taught me anything, it is that normality is not the norm. On average, most people are deeply unusual, and many are even odder than that - I know I am. It's not just that I'm funny looking, my thinking's mental.

But at the end of the day, I'm not the maddest bat in the attic. I once encountered someone whose sanity was so breathtakingly negligible, it was practically subatomic: quantifying it would have required nanotechnology. His name was Nirvana Waddle, and that was just the start of the problem.

I found Nirvana while I was searching for wisdom, and he didn't help much. I admit I was looking in the wrong place, but I had budget issues. I couldn't stretch to the Himalayas, so I'd sought enlightenment in Wales. Now, don't get me wrong, I've always liked Wales. The chapels are lovely places for singsongs, there's no shortage of sheep, and rugby is a bit of a laugh – I do enjoy a good ruck. Brecon's a beacon of hope, but its tepee villages are justifiably under-celebrated.

These crusty reservations lack totem poles, bison, and pow-wows and could only be mistaken for authentic Native American villages by a moron, or perhaps by one of their inhabitants. Still, I had heard tell that a freelance shaman possessing extraordinary unearthly powers dwelt in a tepee near Abergavenny and I had arranged to visit him.

I came equipped with wellies and optimism. Maybe this would be the day that I would gain a deep insight into the meaning of life? After a nineteen-mile trudge through mud, I heard the distant thwack of canvas on wind and knew that I had arrived.

"Welcome to the Owen Glendower Tepee Village!" Nirvana Waddle ejaculated in an effusive Merthyr Tydfil accent. "I know there's only the one tent, but it's a start." The shaman was wearing scarlet sunglasses and a multi-coloured poncho. I had no idea which tribe this signified, but it was not a fashionable one.

The village suffered from a chronic lack of other inhabitants. In fact, I've seen more heavily populated toilet cubicles.

I followed Nirvana to his tepee. The mud was thick, and some of it wasn't mud, but there was no danger of getting lost, what with there only being the one tent. He didn't invite me inside, but at least his awning was wide enough to keep most of the drizzle off. I gingerly positioned my buttocks on his psychedelic welcome mat. It was uncomfortable, but I was tired and didn't particularly care.

Nirvana filled a pair of mugs from a battered pot on his camping stove. "It's ethical coffee," he explained.

The concoction didn't smell ethical. The odour was closer to caffeinated fertilizer, or possibly something worse – human remains, perhaps.

"There's no coffee in it," Nirvana said. "Stimulants are immoral."

I nodded my pretended agreement and attempted a sip.

"It's mostly bracken, acorns and repurposed cow pats," Nirvana said.

I clenched my nostrils and swallowed some gloop. "Delicious. Thanks."

Delighted that his hospitality had been so well received, Nirvana delved into his tepee and dragged out a handwritten sign reading *Shaman For Hire*. "I offer a wide range of services," he explained. "Emotional Enema £33.50, Psychic Detox £48.25, Tantric Gardening £110.75. Tempted? I can photograph your aura if you can keep it still. I've got red-eye reduction..." He paused, waiting expectantly for an answer.

I wanted none of these things. I sought only wisdom.

"Well, have a think about it," Nirvana persisted, "I could really use the work."

As a plea, it was as heartfelt as it was pathetic. Nirvana clearly didn't have much in the way of possessions and he wasn't a householder, he was a tent-holder. As I surveyed his tepee, my gaze landed on a dangling hippie trinket, a gaudy rope lattice suitable for a stoned tarantula. "Nice web," I fibbed.

Nirvana removed the damp artefact. "It's a dreamcatcher."

"What's it used for?"

"It does exactly what it says on the tin."

There wasn't a tin, but I knew what he meant. "How many dreams have you caught?"

"They're countless in number." Nirvana fumbled with the ropey muddle.

"Where do you store them?"

"I've got a set of shelves." Nirvana chuckled.

Nirvana certainly fitted the crusty mould, and he was the kind of bloke many people could never get bored of hitting. But for me, his heart was in the right place, even if his brain wasn't, and he was rumoured to possess the gift of ancient magic.

"What kind of shaman are you?" I asked.

"Freelance," Nirvana replied. "The Revenue won't accept soothsayers as legitimate sole traders and staff jobs are thin on the ground. It's not that I'm insufficiently qualified, neither. I've got a PhD in Unexplained Phenomena from the Portmeirion Institute of Technology. I spent years studying aliens, UFOs, the Rothmans Incident..."

"Wow, what was The Rothmans Incident?"

"Aliens. On YouTube."

"I see." He clearly meant The Roswell Incident, but I caught his drift.

"It's not that I'm short on skills, look you. Bog-standard mystics channel energy. Anyone can do that. But I can channel apathy. Sadly, there's not much call for it round here. The sheep are already sufficiently apathetic, and the farmers can't be bothered."

I could see that circumstances were less than ideal. Tepee villages were better suited to the sultry canyons of the Wild West than the soggy slopes of a Brecon Beacon.

"How did you become a shaman?"

"It's in my blood."

"Your family must be ... special."

"Oh, yes, it made for an interesting childhood, didn't it just. I grew up by the sea, near the bit where the ocean runs out and ships fall off the edge of the world. The sailors' screams kept me awake at night, so my gran would read me Just Not-so Stories - *How The Whale Got Its Arms*, *How The Donkey Got Its Yodel* and *How The Snake Got Its Legs*. I've been confused ever since."

Nirvana went on to explain that although his mammy had an invisible third eye, his father was just a normal bloke who spent his whole life working down a fish mine. After Nirvana had failed all his GCSEs, a mystic career had seemed the best option, and he had been sent to train under a Pontypool mystic known as "Evans of the Middle Pillar". He had completed his training a decade ago and had been hoping to settle down, but Fate had conspired against him. At this point, Nirvana started to become a little emotional. He delved into his poncho and plucked out a completely blue sheet of paper.

"It's a map of Atlantis. Colour-coded." Nirvana used it to wipe his eyes. "I'm anxious about Poppy, my girlfriend, see. We were in a band together - Ocean Colour Finance. They were very now a few years ago. I say girlfriend, but she's really my Spirit Wife. A druid performed a pagan hand-fisting ceremony for us at Stonehenge. But it all started to go wrong when Poppy dropped out of circus school, went travelling and inadvertently unicycled across the Iran-Iraq border. The Foreign Office says they're doing what they can. I've sent friendship bangles to the Shias and the Sunnis, but I haven't heard back yet. If they leave it much longer, I'll send them enemy necklaces."

It was a sorry tale, but I couldn't help thinking that Poppy should have chosen a safer cycle path.

I wondered whether I should unpack some of my own emotional baggage. I wasn't short of divorces, addictions, or criminal convictions, but before I could inflict any of it on Nirvana, he showed me his phone. It was a make I had never seen before, and it was completely dead.

"It's solar powered," Nirvana explained. "Ecologically flawless, but it does mean I can only be contacted outdoors on cloudless days."

I looked up at the murderous Welsh skies and calculated that today at least, he would be contactable for approximately no hours.

A thoughtless silence prevailed, during which I wondered whether I had wasted my time climbing the Brecon Beacons to meet such a shambolic shaman. Eventually, he offered to perform some silent chanting. Never previously having heard silent chanting, I accepted.

Silent chanting proved to be a bit on the uneventful side, and after a few minutes, I'd had enough.

Nirvana showed me how to realign my chakras, then expounded at length about Thoth, an Egyptian *tarot* pronounced like a speech impediment, and his emotional kinship with the Greek gods "Apollo, Diabetes and Hepatitis".

I quizzed him for all I was worth, trying to divine the mysteries of the universe, but his answers were as straight and direct as a Welsh road and, after an hour or two of scrambled mythology, I was none the wiser.

I couldn't leave without learning something, so I asked Nirvana what, besides emotional enemas, psychic detoxes, and tantric gardening, he had on offer.

He shuffled towards me and spoke in a low, confidential voice. It was completely unnecessary, given that we were the only humans for miles, but with Nirvana, paranoia and shamanism seemed to go hand in hand: "I could give you an OBE."

"A medal?"

"An Out-of-Body Experience."

I didn't have a particularly enviable body, given its age and shape, but I did find it useful.

I hesitated.

"Go on," he insisted. "It'll blow your mind. I'll do it for half price."

"How much?"

"Eighty quid."

"So, it's forty."

"No, it's eighty after I've halved it."

I had come a long way and I figured that, if I dodged the fare on the train home, I could probably afford it.

Nirvana took my money, retreated to his tepee, and returned with a concoction so noxious, it made the ethical coffee taste like champagne.

After I had sunk it, Nirvana chanted noises reminiscent of the climactic battle in Planet of the Apes, then began to speak with calm intensity: "You are not you. You are other to yourself. Rise up, rise up, and see what you are."

I felt lighter and my perspective lifted until I could look down on my own bald patch. I hadn't realised how extensive it had become. It was no longer a small fleshy island in a sea of hair, it was more like a continent of exposed skin encircled by a narrow follicle moat. Then, without warning, my point of view took flight, and I was looking down on the Brecon Beacons from a passing raincloud. Was this what happened when you died? I gazed at the dank mountains, the sheep, the barren nothingness, and marvelled. Had I been reincarnated as drizzle? Or was I now an all-seeing, all-knowing divinity able to witness human affairs with supine detachment? Either way, it was freezing, damp, and lonely. There were no human affairs to witness, and if I was drizzle, I couldn't wait to fall. When you are in your body, it's much easier to go places. Stuck up here, outside my body, the possibilities were much more limited. I wondered what was keeping me up. Was I gliding on a thermal? Had Nirvana pressed a celestial pause button? There was no one to ask. It struck me as strange that humanity had spent so long dreaming of flight, when there was so much more going on at ground level. If only the shaman had provided an in-flight movie and a drinks trolley. Just when I was ready to scream with boredom, and die of out-of-body hypothermia, my perspective swooped down like a kestrel preying on a dormouse. It was *Hello Bald Patch!* then back inside my skin.

"How was that?" Nirvana asked.

"Well, it worked," I replied.

"Told you it would," Nirvana said. "Fancy doing it again?"

"No, ta." I thanked him and headed for the station. Somehow, fare-dodging in my body was a more attractive prospect than flying out of it.

RULE 13 - REVENGE IS A DISH BEST SERVED BY A VOODOO PRIESTESS

I once stumbled across a voodoo shop near the North Circular Road. I had no idea what I wanted, having neither visited Haiti nor cast a spell, but I had just been banned from IKEA for the fourth time and was keen to embrace a new consumer experience.

I don't know what kind of customer service I had anticipated, but the beefy, Oxbridge type behind the counter was not it. I waited for him to serve a cheerful traffic warden a packet of *Satan Begone* incense sticks and a pot of *Luv Luv Oil*, then tentatively approached the counter.

The shopkeeper explained that *Zombie Sorcery* was the finest voodoo shop within walking distance of the A406. People simply couldn't get enough of *Rattlesnake Root*, *Necromancy Powder*, and *High John the Conqueror* deodorant. His line in pet spells was particularly popular: a pack of *Sovereign of the Cemeteries* pellets could de-worm a Jack Russell in minutes, a handful of *Wahoo Bark* sprinklings could bring goldfish back from the dead and a slice or two of *Devil Shoestring Root* could dissolve feline fur-balls in under a fortnight.

Frankly, he had me at *Necromancy Powder*. I simply had to find out more, and given that there were no other customers, he was happy to oblige. The bloke told me his name was Rob and he dug out a couple of zombie-themed deckchairs. Rob explained that he had grown up in Surrey, played prop forward for Westminster, read PPE at Balliol then trained in broadcast media. He had harboured dreams of becoming a foreign correspondent and reporting bravely under shellfire, but the channel's Head of Diversity and Inclusion, an old-Etonian viscount with his own grouse moor, had nabbed his girlfriend, then made him redundant on the grounds that he no longer fitted their "employability criteria" and needed to "check his privilege". This had all seemed a bit rich from a bloke who was more than a bit rich, but there was nothing he could do about it, other than get a new career and a new home.

Rob felt numb and disillusioned, so he scoured the job sites for something he could approach with total indifference. Many of the opportunities on offer required dedication and enthusiasm, but when he found a producer vacancy on a daytime pet-care show only available on a four-figure channel number, he knew he had struck mediocrity gold. Further inquiry revealed that the job came with free accommodation in the co-presenter's attic, so it was a no-brainer.

Whilst I sympathised with Rob, I could not figure out what any of this had to do with voodoo. Noting my puzzlement, he brewed us some ginger tea and assured me that everything he had told me was essential to understanding his initiation into the mysteries of Haiti. As he related his tale, he spoke with the cultivated air of a World Service newsreader and the calm demeanour of a man who has enacted vengeance and secured peace of mind:

***

"I had the feeling I was the only candidate for the job," Rob explained, "so, the interview call was over in a couple of minutes. I chucked most of my stuff in storage, bunged my essentials into a rucksack and headed for a comfortably dull area of North London.

My new landlady rejoiced in the name Waspy Glyndebourne. She had the complexion of Ben Nevis, the stature of Tyson Fury and all the feminine vulnerability of Wormwood Scrubs. At eighty-one, six-feet-four and fifteen stone, she could have renamed herself *HMS Glyndebourne*. Her arms were like pile drivers, she had the fists of a Neanderthal prize fighter, and her voice was so forceful it could have arm-wrestled Priti Patel. She wasn't just ballsy: she had metaphorical testicles bulging out of her proverbial trouser legs.

Her living room walls pulsated in time to *The Archers*. A hearing aid would have been out of the question, she explained - if she was becoming deaf, the rest of the world would simply have to shout. The environmental health officers who had recently acted on a complaint about the volume of *The Shipping Forecast* could do their worst; she'd survived Haiti, after all. If she could cope with hurricanes and the homicidal dictator *Papa Doc* Duvalier, a few local bureaucrats presented little opposition.

Waspy offered an induction, beginning with a thirty-minute demonstration of her alarm system. She explained that the code was only seven digits long and could be easily memorised as the year of the Battle of Bosworth followed by the number of chapters in Psalms. Escape involved grappling with six chains, two Chubb locks and a Yale. Failure to unlock them in the correct order would set off a system of sirens and revolving blue lights. I couldn't understand why Waspy was so terrified of burglars. If she'd pinned a photograph of herself on her front gate and labelled it, *I Live Here*, it would have scared off the bravest cartel in Mexico.

Waspy's wallpaper was a floral Guernica: grotesque botanical abominations in pink, apricot and purple, all punctuated by anaemic watercolours of yachts. Every ornament commemorated a failed royal marriage and the novelty barometers covering the hall walls made a variety of contradictory forecasts. On the way upstairs, Waspy explained that all the clocks in the house were twenty minutes fast because "punctuality was the practice of princes".

After the fifth flight, we reached my new attic flat and Waspy conducted a brief tour. Apart from the rather wonky en-suite toilet, everything was Haitian: zombie dolls dangled from the ceiling like sinister stalactites; and metalwork sculptures of mermaids, snakes, dragons, and angels lurked in every corner. A wooden chair was carved with an elaborate cockfight and there were framed sketches of cemeteries and iron gravestone crosses nailed to the walls. Power cuts wouldn't have been a problem, as there were human skull candles to send back evil, inflammatory confusion candles to break hexes, and wormwood candles to recruit the help of the dead. There was a miniature botanical garden of weird plants with names like *Cruel Man of the Woods*, *Ladies Thumb* and *Five Finger Root*, and an array of boxes containing powders, implements, and emergency supplies of *Wahoo Bark,* bottles of *Jezebel Oil*, *Fast Luck Incense*, and a stuffed jar of *Waste Away Tea*.

"Make yourself at home," Waspy said, with a generous sweep of her arm.

At any other point in my life, I would have left without further shilly-shallying, but I was heartbroken and genuinely didn't care.

Waspy was clearly bonkers, but so what? The world was unhinged, so why shouldn't my flat be too?

I unpacked onto the bed. The sheets were blood-red, and the duvet was emblazoned with Haitian werewolves, but at least it matched the decor.

I went downstairs for a welcoming dinner. Waspy called it "homemade sushi", but it was just batter-less fish fingers on congealed rice pudding. After I had complimented Waspy on her cooking and consumed some of it, she poured me a large Haitian rum and celebrated my new tenancy with some indoor fireworks. Small snakes of carbon uncoiled themselves onto saucers; coloured knobs went *phut* in bowls and a Catherine wheel the size of a ball-bearing rotated in a dish.

There was a knock at the door. Waspy swore in Haitian and bounded out of her armchair with the force of a veteran pentathlete. Chains were unleashed and a canine killing machine jumped up at my chest with a petrifying growl.

"Slobodan's only playing," Waspy reassured me.

I froze to the spot and managed to whisper, "Good boy," but it probably sounded more like, "Goodbye."

"Slobodan's a girl, you fool!" Waspy boomed. "There was a little confusion at her christening, but never mind that now. Don't let her know you're frightened, man! She'll smell it and I won't be responsible for the consequences."

Suitably reassured, I tried not to relax my bowels. Waspy left the room and a rotund lady with bulging facial veins entered clutching a lead. She introduced herself as Waspy's co-presenter, Aurora Thumper-Brithazard, and launched into an impromptu diatribe about Slobodan: "She's had a difficult enough day. I was trying to mate her with another tri-colour pit bull, and they were far from willing to commence proceedings, so we both had to get down on all fours and simulate the desired action. It took three hours and aggravated the arthritis in my left knee as well as making Slobodan cry. She's very loyal, a lovely dog; murdered her first-born, mind you, but nobody's perfect."

I tried to reverse gently away from Slobodan, but the beast followed me, keeping her paws on my chest.

Waspy returned with a toothbrush and bucket. "Mind making yourself useful, my boy? Slobodan's dental hygiene's been far from immaculate of late - shocking halitosis. Make sure you give her incisors a good scrub."

I stroked the dog tentatively and somehow gathered the courage to part its lips; lion tamers would have blanched. As I did this, Waspy started banging on about declining grammar standards in the local graffiti and how this marked the end of western civilisation. I was pretending to agree when Slobodan bit into the toothbrush and pulled it out of my hand, waving her massive head from side to side in a frantic motion.

Waspy thumped the coffee table. Its legs shuddered: when Waspy thumped a table, it stayed thumped. The shock startled Slobodan and she began to wheeze. At this, Waspy's expression turned to that of an affronted Old Testament God. "Damn you! I'll have to get Slobodan her inhaler now, you've aggravated her asthma." She took Slobodan in her muscular arms, stroked her head, and began to sing a Haitian Creole lullaby into its left ear.

It was a grotesque sight, made even more disturbing by the tiny headless doll dangling from Waspy's necklace. I made my excuses and headed up to the comforts of my werewolf duvet.

I can't say I slept well, but it didn't really matter. Even though I was starting a new job, failure was of no consequence whatever.

HOW NOT TO LIVE YOUR LIFE

The daytime pet-care show was called *We Are All Bunnies*, and it was recorded in a basement at the wrong end of Colindale. The studio had never been soundproofed, so sirens and shouts punctuated proceedings at intervals. It often fell out of sync, lending it the quality of a poorly dubbed Brazilian soap opera and the cameras were operated by unpaid work experiencers. The programme was an insult to the inventors of moving pictures. Had he seen *We Are All Bunnies*, William Horner would have un-invented the Zoetrope, the Lumière Brothers would have left their train in its siding, D.W. Griffith would have aborted his Nation, Eisenstein would have anchored Potemkin and Hitchcock would have pulled himself together and stopped being so morbid.

On the whole, the animal contributors to *We Are All Bunnies* were far better adjusted than the human ones. Whereas the former suffered from a variety of more-or-less minor physical ailments, the humans tended to rejoice in a broad variety of incurable psychological defects. The adored pet compensated for the hollowness of a marriage, the absence of a child, the pain of social isolation, an empty retirement, a recent divorce, or an unexpected bereavement.

One time, an old codger came to the studio. He was well-dressed, well-spoken, and desperate for advice. The problem was, his two Jack Russell Terriers simply couldn't get on. They fought all the time, and it was driving him completely hatstand. Waspy asked him why he had only brought one dog to the studio, and he looked utterly bewildered. She held up a single finger, and asked, "How many fingers have I got up?" When he replied, "Two", no further diagnosis was required. Double vision can be a cruel affliction.

That evening, I went for a quick five k. I ran along reassuringly named roads like *Vale of Health* and *Well Walk*, and it was all expensively pseudo-rural. This was the kind of district where the police were most often called out to enforce hosepipe bans. People walked along the pavements reading books or cycled along listening to classical music from transistor radios strapped to their baskets and, although the narrow streets had been designed for carriages, all the cars seemed to be four-wheel drives.

I stopped a couple of minutes short of the house and rested on a bench to check my phone. There was a notification – my nemesis was about to make a speech to the Royal Television Society about "diversity, equality and inclusion". I looked at the viscount's hypocritical face, swore extensively then headed back to my new home.

I undid the triple lock, struggled to recall the year of the Battle of Bosworth and the number of chapters in Psalms, then found to my relief that the alarm was off. Downstairs was as silent as a cemetery, but as I ascended the stairs, I became aware of a clumping noise and a strange background hum. I wondered whether Waspy was hoovering, but as I climbed higher up, it became increasingly clear that this would have to have been with a very strange brand of vacuum cleaner indeed.

As I approached the attic, the sounds became clearer, but more mystifying. There was an otherworldly wailing and a kind of rhythmic stamping. It was so unnerving, I felt forced to conduct a recce via my en-suite toilet. With its low, sloping ceiling, it was an inconvenient convenience, and it had a high window ludicrously positioned to look out onto my bedroom. I clambered onto the toilet seat, leant sideways and gripped a pipe, allowing me to see what was causing the commotion.

Sometimes, there's a thin line between laughing and screaming and, at that moment, I trod this as precariously as a rhino on a high wire. My octogenarian landlady was in her pants, conducting a voodoo rite with Aurora and Slobodan. Smoke billowed while Waspy performed a Haitian form of the can-can and Aurora made various unpleasant noises with improbable instruments, but it was Slobodan, sat howling in the corner of a flour circle, who was the centre of attention. Waspy waved things into the dog's face, chanted into its floppy ears and pointed at its nose with a peculiar stick.

I was dumbstruck; it was partly shock, but mostly, it was fear. This was in no way decreased when Slobodan began to speak in a voice that seemed uncannily deep for a bitch: "Who dares to summon me?"

"I damn well do, you poltroon, the Voodoo Queen of Hampstead Garden Suburb!" Waspy continued her can-can as she spoke, alternating words with high kicks. "Tell us who on earth you are and don't beat around the bush."

Slobodan's mouth moved, and the bass voice continued, "I inhabit the dog you have before you."

"Who are you and what are you doing in my dog?" Waspy demanded.

"My name's Norman and I used to be a management consultant," the possessed dog replied. "I liked to go potholing at weekends and one time I dropped my inhaler into an underground stream. The worry brought on an asthma attack, and I kicked the proverbial bucket before I'd had a chance to spot any decent stalactites. My body was never found, so I now roam the world as a spirit hiding in various dogs."

"Why dogs?"

"I like dogs. I always wanted to own one. They have a good life, dogs, chasing things and napping, but the trouble is, I do tend to give them asthma; it's very trying."

"Oh, the heart simply bleeds. Pathetic! Lily-livered pansy! You're thinking only of yourself. Imagine what this poor animal has been through. Now, away with you before I put a curse on your departed soul."

"But..."

"That's quite enough. Now, naff off!"

"Alright then, if you insist."

"I damn well do insist! Dead management consultants are all the same, self-obsessed loonies the lot of you!"

"See you, then." the spirit said, as Slobodan's breathing returned to normal.

The smoke evaporated, Aurora stopped making strange musical sounds, and, to my horror, my mobile rang. I scrabbled around inside my track suit with the desperation of a man looking for an unexploded grenade. I had to do this one-handed, as my grip on the overhead pipe was the only thing preventing me toppling off the toilet. I managed to kill the call before the third ring, but the effort made the overhead pipe come off in my hand, and I crashed onto the floor. Noxious fluid shot out of the pipe, redecorating the bathroom, and making enough noise to wake the dead and alert the neighbouring zombie-botherers.

Slobodan growled, heavy footsteps thundered, and my panty-clad landlady peered down at me through the window, saying, "Oh. You," in a tone of disappointment.

"Bit of a plumbing problem, Waspy," I stammered. "Have it fixed in no time." I tried to force the pipe back into place, diverting the fluid up my nostrils.

A forearm that would not have disgraced Popeye the Sailor Man reached through the window and wrenched the pipe back into place.

"Thanks, Waspy."

"Let's reconvene for a house meeting once you've cleaned up and packed."

So, I was being evicted by a voodoo priestess for a minor bathroom accident. As I mopped up, changed, and gathered up my gear, I riled at the injustice of it all.

Downstairs, Waspy and Aurora were sat listening to *You and Yours* at stadium rock volume. Waspy poured me a large rum from a bottle labelled with werewolves and gestured towards an armchair.

"You must be terribly confused, but there really is absolutely nothing whatsoever to worry about. I am indeed a voodoo priestess or *mambo*, if you will, but it's all perfectly normal," Waspy paused. "In Haiti."

I was sure it was and said so very quietly.

"You see, I was based out in Haiti for years with a dull little husband and one simply had to find ways to pass the time. Voodoo was the natural choice and it's come in quite handy ever since, particularly with pets. Aurora helps me keep my hand in, and she's a rather gifted musician."

"You're extremely talented," I told Aurora, meekly.

"So," Waspy concluded. "There's really nothing to worry about. Everything's completely above board."

I decided to ask the improbable but unavoidable question, "Why were you exorcising your dog?"

"Oh, she's had a touch of asthma for yonks, ridiculous really in a fighting dog. Anyway, I usually find with most veterinary complaints that it boils down to voodoo exorcism. A quick invocation, a bit of a jig in my knickers, give the invading spirit a stern talking to, and they bugger off sharpish, along with the ailments. Vets should try voodoo more often."

"Does voodoo have any other uses at all?" I asked, a touch disingenuously.

"Oh, bags of things. Bringing luck, getting rich, staying healthy, curing the mad, diabolical curses, exacting revenge, you name it. Jolly useful if you ask me. Anything I can help you with? I appreciate that I caused you a little stress and, I'm afraid I don't think we're going to be able to work together terribly well after this. You know my secret and I'm perfectly willing to let you live but seeing you every day to discuss mildly unwell gerbils might be a little awkward. I'm sure Aurora feels the same."

"Yes, dear." Aurora gave me a kindly smile.

I wanted to leave, but an irresistible idea took hold of both my mind and mouth. "Given that I'll keep this to myself and leave quietly, might you be able to see your way to helping me out with a small personal matter?"

I told her about the viscount who had ended my career. It tickled her interest and, once I had shown her his picture and the details of his imminent Royal Television Society speech, she said, "There's no time like the present!" and giggled like the world's heftiest schoolgirl. "I haven't had a chance to cast any decent spells for absolutely ages! Fancy a spot of the old mumbo-jumbo, Aurora? A little more spirit bothering for my soon-to-be-ex lodger? Least we can do in return for him keeping shtum, I would have thought. What do you say?"

Aurora put on her slippers and said, "That would be lovely."

We headed back upstairs to the attic, tidied up the remnants of Slobodan's exorcism, and prepared to enact voodoo vengeance on the viscount.

While I set up a live stream of the Royal Television Society event on my laptop, Waspy and Aurora gathered mystical materials from the boxes.

"Where did we put the *Necromancy Powder*?" Waspy enquired.

"There you go, dear," Aurora replied.

Waspy scooped white powder from a box engraved with vampires, set light to it and, within seconds, billows of white smoke were filling the room.

"Pass me the Satan's Ram," Waspy asked, as casually as if she were saying, "Pass the salt".

Aurora reached into a box carved with serpents and produced a chunky candle. "There you go, High Priestess."

"Staff of Moses." Waspy could have been a surgeon in a Haitian edition of *M*A*S*H*.

Aurora passed her a large wooden stick carved into the shape of a striking viper.

"Now, be a good chap and hold this between your teeth." Waspy passed me a small scroll. "And do try not to salivate. It damages the paper. Oh, and if you wouldn't mind, wave this about every so often." Waspy passed me a flag embroidered with zombies. "Now, hang on a minute while I invoke *Erzulie, Goddess of Love*, *Mademoiselle Brigitte, Guardian of the Graves* and *Ogou Balanjo, Spirit of Healing*."

Waspy lit an assortment of candles and chucked flour around the room for a few minutes. "Now, would you mind scattering a little of this Graveyard Dust, Aurora?"

"Consider it done, old bean."

Waspy passed me two stones. She explained that they were lodestones and that I was to hold the red one in my right hand and the white one in my left. She then gave me some final maternal advice. "Now, young man, *The Great Serpent* will shortly be dancing in your head. Be jolly careful."

I agreed that I would take care.

"I can't predict what will happen," Waspy continued. "But when you see the perpetrator of your injustice, just mention my full title - *The Voodoo Queen of Hampstead Garden Suburb* – and the vengeance will begin."

I turned to the live feed on my laptop. The aristocratic Head of Diversity and Inclusion had mounted the podium and was spouting forth about "unconscious bias", "allyship" and "transparency". But he hadn't counted on the inclusion of anything as diverse as Waspy Glyndebourne.

I did as Waspy had instructed, and said, "The Voodoo Queen of Hampstead Garden Suburb".

Waspy chanted an invocation, "*Au nom Monsieur Damballah-Wedo-Toka-Miorwaze.*" The repetitive rhythm became increasingly hypnotic and the elderly but powerfully built pet care specialist began to dance, kicking her legs shoulder-high like a *Moulin Rouge* barnstormer.

At intervals, Aurora shook a snake's backbone rattle, beat a small drum, and bugled flatulently on a conch shell. Waspy's kicks became increasingly extreme until dislocation was a genuine risk and I worried for the lampshade. Finally, Waspy collapsed onto the floor with a shriek and her eyeballs bulged to bursting point. Aurora increased the rapidity of her drumming and honking to a frantic pace while Waspy flailed around the carpet shrieking like a breakdancing demon.

As the ritual built to a pitch, Waspy leapt up, banging her head on the ceiling. But she was beyond pain. Something powerful and Haitian inhabited her, and she spoke in a deep masculine voice as she repeated the incantation, "*Au nom Monsieur Damballah-Wedo-Toka-Miorwaze.*".

The Viscount's Diversity and Inclusion speech had reached the words, "We must show empathy for the marginalized," when he began to dance like a chicken, elbows pumping rhythmically, knees bent, head pecking backwards and forward. There were gasps, giggles, and murmurs from the four hundred-odd delegates, and these only increased as he embarked on the most contorted song I had ever heard, every word a monstrous parody of itself: Meeeeee Toooooo, Traaaaaaaans Wwwwwwomen Are Reeeeeeeeeal Wwwwwwwwomen, Chchchchchchchcheck

Yoooooooour Priviledggggggge. He could not have infused more contempt into each phrase if he'd inserted every swear word in existence and projected them onto a nude image of Donald Trump. The indignant audience began to shout in outrage. Walkouts began.

The speaker continued his chicken dance whilst reciting contorted gender pronouns in a series of contemptuous clucks and squawks:

"Zzzzzzzzieself! Cluck!"

"Verselfffffff! Squawk!"

"Emmmmmmmmmself! Cluck!"

Once he had reached number seventy-four, the smoke evaporated, Waspy stopped breakdancing, and Aurora stopped bugling on her conch shell.

I checked my Twitter feed. The viscount was trending – "He should hang his beak in shame!", "Diversity chicken should get stuffed", "Cancel the Viscount."

I punched the air. "Got the bastard!"

"Damn well did it!" Waspy offered a hi-five. "The old mumbo-jumbo works every time."

***

His curious tale of dogs, possession, and diversity and inclusion policies complete, Rob poured me some more ginger tea and explained that the voodoo vengeance had turned out to be the start of a beautiful friendship. Waspy had shared her wealth of Haitian contacts in return for a share of his new retail venture, and he had soon established himself as the North Circular's public face of voodoo. Britain may be a nation of shopkeepers, he explained, but a select few are supplied by Haiti.

I thanked him for his time and was about to leave when a thought crossed my mind: could I inflict voodoo vengeance on a local Scandinavian superstore?

RULE 14 - REALITY IS OVERRATED

I once met a woman who lived in a skip; it was love at first sight. This was no ordinary skip – it was layered, like an inedible pie. The crust comprised a rotten mattress, a manual lawnmower, a one-handed clock, a stringless banjo, and a rusty *Unclaimed Baggage* sign. At first, there was nothing to indicate that the skip was inhabited, but after I had spent twenty minutes resting against it drinking cider out of a bag, it birthed a young woman. She emerged like a swamp monster but wasn't covered in slime. Her off-yellow jacket, stripy t-shirt and once-luminous dungarees reminded me of a faded rainbow.

She seemed grateful for the company and introduced herself as *Camden Lock Nessie*. There was a certain logic to this – the skip was near London's Camden Lock Market and Nessie was one way of shortening what turned out to be her name, Vanessa. But there wasn't much logic to anything else about her.

"I am as barking as a tub of Rottweilers," she explained, after minimal formalities had been exchanged. "Sometimes, I see voices.

They use sign language". She turned to the empty space beside her and screamed, "Shut up, Kevin!" before turning back to me. "Kevin's my imaginary enemy. Bastard."

We stood there for a bit as she strummed the stringless banjo. It may have woven entrancing melodies in her imagination, but it did very little for me. When she'd finished, she said, "If all the world's a stage, then schizophrenics play many parts, often simultaneously."

I had not often heard this point of view expressed before. She really did seem to have a new take on the universe, albeit a deranged one.

"I've had a hard old fantasy life," she continued. "I've been places no one else has seen. Invisible places. In my head."

I couldn't help but wonder how someone so well-travelled had ended up in a skip, so I asked her as delicately as I could.

She didn't dwell on the details. "Some people are driven. But I'm parked. Probably by demons." At that, she leant back a little too far and fell back on the abandoned mattress. "Sorry about that. I've got leaning difficulties." She laughed hysterically, a sort of cockney wheeze. As Nessie recovered her position, she grabbed the one-handed clock and said, "That'll come in handy! It'll help me keep track of the seconds."

I wondered what time meant to someone like Nessie. How did she spend it? Surely the contents of her skip offered limited possibilities.

"Hope you don't mind me asking, but what do you do all day?"

"History," Nessie replied.

"How do you mean?"

"I shoplift history books."

"Do you read them?"

"No, I cook them."

"Oh. What do they taste like?"

"Course I bleedin' read them! Why else would I nick them?"

"I've always liked history," I lied.

"There's a lot to like and a lot to hate. Either way, there's a lot of it."

"I know what you mean." I didn't.

"History helps me understand what's going on," she said. "Especially in my head." Reacting to a noise only she could hear, Nessie dropped the clock. "Shush! Napoleon's trying to whisper something." She turned and listened intently to the invisible Emperor of the French. "Never... You're not having me on now are you, Bonaparte? ... Well, I never." She turned back to me. "Apparently, Primrose Hill's about to erupt. It's lain dormant for a suspiciously long time, so I'd steer well clear if you don't want to get covered in pumice." She turned back to Napoleon. "Thanks for the tip-off, Emperor."

Primrose Hill was a few minutes' walk away. The grassy, sixty-metre bump boasted an excellent view of London Zoo but Vesuvius, it wasn't.

"There's no obvious explanation for the regular misbehaviour of my head," Nessie continued. "Sometimes, life speeds up and colours itself in. At other times, it makes geology look pacy."

I sympathised. Existence could be problematic.

"I know I'm a few Rizlas short of the proverbial spliff," she said. "Sometimes, it even feels like someone's translated reality into a language I can't speak and I'm searching for the subtitles."

I wanted to put an arm on her shoulder. Having your head turn against you could not be easy.

"Suicide is self-defeating," Nessie said. "Yesterday, I tried to gas myself in an electric oven. Couple of months back, I overdosed on laxatives. That stank." Once again, she laughed like a malfunctioning pneumatic drill. "I've not had a good day. I was late for my voice-hearers support group. I ran as fast as I could hobble, but I fell down a manhole and landed on a man. Nice bloke. Gave me a leg up and I wasn't too late for the clinic. The doctor calls us his *joyful little mysteries*. He wants to create an *oasis of respect* where we can *express our unmet needs*. Patronizing knob. "Good news," he says the other day. "We've stabilized your instability." Well, forgive me if I don't ululate. The nurses just tell me to "get some rest" and "read *Revelations*". I tried, but it wasn't a recipe for sanity: "The City of the Seven Hills will be utterly destroyed, and a thousand multi-headed frog-beasts shall devour the sky." You're better off watching *The One Show*."

I took her point. The bible had a long-established relationship with insanity. I mentioned this and she told me a story about two psychiatric patients she had once known. One thought he was God, the other thought he was Jesus, and when they had first met, things had looked a bit tense for a while, until the one who thought he was Jesus said, "Dad!", and the one who thought he was God said, "Son!" and they'd embraced.

We laughed at this oddly life-affirming anecdote for a few seconds, but Nessie appeared to be gripped by an unseen terror. Some beguiling Spirit of Nonsense had descended upon her, and she seemed to be gazing on a distant horizon, many miles from Camden.

Nessie explained that she had a problem. Although she may look like a homeless woman from the early twenty-first century, she was actually a concubine from medieval Istanbul and Sultan Ibrahim The Mad, his Chief Black Eunuch and eighteen Nubian giants were chasing her. By smuggling in an unsliced cucumber, she had polluted the purity of the sultan's harem and now faced execution by being bound hand and foot, sewn up in a sack and drowned.

It seemed unlikely, but I was happy to offer comfort to one of the world's most strangely afflicted. She jumped out of the skip, grabbed my hand, and dragged me through the streets of Camden with feverish force. Lurid polystyrene heads dangled menacingly from the front of shops offering inflatable furniture, juggling accessories, fur-framed mirrors, clockwork Hindu Gods, sun-bleached lesbian pornography, and suspiciously young antiques. A window sign declared, *We Do Not Pierce Belly Buttons, Nor Do We Know A Place That Does*. There were wailing street musicians high on meths and blanket-shaking prophets; a man in a torn business suit attempted to destroy a parked car with an invisible weapon, a screaming pensioner threw eggs at a bus shelter and a three-legged dog bounced improbably along the pavement.

Camden seemed to be crammed with people who would list their hobbies as "traffic baiting", "aggressive mumbling", and "solo boxing". Every one of them was the life and soul of their own imaginary party. A young man lay on the pavement, warbling on a recycled didgeridoo and a beetroot-tinted woman sang, "Gin! Give me some gin! I want some gin! Gin!" There was a plaintive lilt to her wailing that was practically an invitation to homicide.

The street stalls' odours inflicted brutal olfactory violence. Fried pizza slabs, burgers of dubious provenance, tortured lentils, incense, urine, petrol, and trampled vegetables combined into a poisonous potpourri. The whole postal district was several months past its sell-by date.

We dodged two white Rastafarians trying to sell us sun-dried raisins as cannabis resin and ran into the market. Stalls offered artisan water, stolen socks, made-to-measure massage tables, lava lamps, plasma balls, velvet capes and Native American tarot cards.

Nessie was running as though her life depended on it and, in her head, it did. "Quick! I don't want to get chucked in the Bosporus!"

We concealed ourselves behind a vintage cereal stall, and Nessie expanded on her imaginary predicament. If she surrendered there'd be no point begging for mercy - the Sultan was not a reasonable man.

He had been imprisoned for twenty-two years, the last four in the palace cage with only mutes for companions and porn for intellectual enlightenment. On his release, he had followed the Ottoman Code of Fratricide by strangling all twenty-eight of his brothers with a handkerchief. He had been drinking throughout a week-long circumcision feast and was now more than ready to take it out on a rebellious concubine.

Nessie's entirely illusory time in Istanbul's four-hundred-room harem had, she said, been tiring to say the least. Sultan Ibrahim The Mad was determined to mark his name in history by inventing as many new sexual positions as possible and had covered the harem's walls and ceilings with mirrors to observe his couplings and triplings from a variety of angles. Ibrahim neighed like a stallion throughout his vigorous trysting and forced all his concubines to wear clothes held together with an adhesive that melted gradually at room temperature. Being guarded twenty-four hours a day by eighteen Nubian slaves had also been rather testing. When they weren't bickering about camel wrestling, they were making obscene jokes about their sultan's appetites, and even though they were all heavily armed and of intimidating stature, they were each named after different varieties of tulip.

This was all very well, but we were in Camden Market, one of London's smelliest tourist attractions. I pointed this out as tactfully as I could, but she wasn't having it: we were deep within the labyrinths and arcaded courtyards of Medieval Istanbul's Spice Bazaar, where merchants were busy selling belly-dancers, mechanical nightingales and performing dwarves. I could see no evidence of any of these things, but I couldn't leave Nessie alone with her delusions, particularly given how much I fancied her.

Eventually, we were discovered cowering behind the vintage cereal stall, not by an enraged sultan, but by a tall, frail drunk in his late seventies. He was the colour of nicotine: even his coat and beard were faded yellow, and he held a plastic bag the shade of rotting daffodils. After staring at us for a bit, he flourished a plastic crucifix in front of his furrowed face and mumbled a heartfelt blessing.

It would have been nice if it had worked, but it didn't. Nessie remained under her delusion's spell and dragged me back outside. Whatever I said to reassure her, road signs transformed under Nessie's gaze into gilded imperial monograms, newsagents became kiosks of pearl and marble, and wailing street musicians became the Ottoman court's expert lutenists and harpists.

In some ways, Nessie's imagined world was a better place than the reality I inhabited. The cash points at Camden's World's End crossroads each had two queues: the shorter ones were for cash withdrawal; the longer ones were for bearded men demanding money from the first queue.

Nessie explained that Ibrahim The Mad, his Chief Black Eunuch and the eighteen Nubian slaves were almost upon us. Two of the slaves had produced woman-sized sacks and were waving them about their heads as they chanted one of their sultan's hunting poems.

I suggested we escape by nipping on the tube. We went down the escalator and took the High Barnet Branch. Nessie clutched my hand as we sat in silence. I enjoyed her company. She had a mysterious fourth dimension, inhabiting unseen worlds and hearing silent voices. It didn't do her any good, but it did make her interesting. After three stops, we arrived at Archway, she leapt to her feet and ran out of the carriage without letting go.

I was pretty sure that it had been somewhere around here that a defeated Dick Whittington had turned again before becoming thrice Lord Mayor of London. If the venerable Dick had repeated the action at the start of the third millennium, he would have seen that the streets of London were paved, not with gold, but with comatose schizophrenics, used condoms and dog excrement. Dick Whittington would probably have turned yet again and continued out of London.

Nessie seemed intent on going up the hill and scaling Archway Bridge. With an eighty-foot drop onto the trunk road below, it has often proven a popular spot for exiting the world, and I was keen that Nessie's despair didn't drive her into taking this option. This might have been easier had she not been somewhere else entirely in her head. Where most people heard the accumulated engine rumbles of the A1 in rush hour, Nessie said she discerned the whispering waves of the Bosporus. They seemed to be calling out to her, crashing on the shore with a murmured "Vanessa, Vanessa, Vanessa."

We looked out through the heat haze and petrol vapour shadows at what I thought was The Shard, The Gherkin, and Canary Wharf, and what Nessie believed to be Istanbul's Blue Mosque, Executioner's Fountain, and Gates of Felicity. Closer at hand, a grim seventeen-storey DSS building was, to her, the spectacular Topkapi Palace, home to the Ottoman Empire for twenty-one generations.

The Nubian slaves were getting louder in Nessie's head. She could hear their chanting, the swish of their scimitars, and the swirling of their sacks. She turned North, and pointed out The Bosporus, The Sea of Marmara, and The Golden Horn. The Ottoman fleet was moored across the bay, she said, and the royal barge was a few hundred feet beneath us.

Three joggers approached, all earnest, heavy-bellied men in bulging Lycra. To me, they could not have been much less threatening. To Nessie, they were the Sultan and his men, about to drown her in a sack.

"No! They'll never take me!" With unnerving athleticism, Nessie clambered up the railings, raised her arms into a diving position, and prepared to leap off the bridge. Her body was backlit by the sun like an all-embracing halo, marking her passage into another world.

"Wait!" I shouted and unleashed my best bar-fighting skills on the runners. It's not hard to deck fat fitness freaks when they're not expecting it.

Nessie climbed back off the railings and hugged me. "My hero!".

And reader, I married her.

RULE 15 - WHAT GOES AROUND COMES AROUND, BUT SOME PEOPLE DUCK

I once met a brilliant moron: ideas of an Einstein, sense of a toddler. People called him Chewie, partly on account of his wild ginger hair, unkempt beard, and gangly limbs but mostly because he was a total space cadet.

We were the only customers in Wolverhampton's worst pub, and he looked like a man with a story to tell. I stood him a stout and he explained that, until recently, he had enjoyed a successful career in the tech sector, launching a galaxy of gizmos onto global markets. He loved his work and had even been profiled in *Wired Magazine*, but in the space of a fortnight, he had not only lost his job he had lost a planet.

I sympathised as best I could. Over the years, I had lost my share of jobs, women, and keys. Mislaying a planet had to hurt.

Chewie offered to talk me through his demise. Failure is right up my street, so I was delighted to accept. As he told his sorry tale, Chewie's stout foamed his beard, making him a potential contender for the world's worst Santa, but I tried not to let this detract from the gravitas of his personal tragedy.

He began with the collapse of his career, partly because it happened first, and partly because he was still mourning the mislaid planet and needed to build up to it gently:

***

"It all went wrong in Birmingham," he began. "I was in a conference hall, addressing a visiting delegation of Chinese business leaders. These guys held the keys to a market of 1.45 billion people. That's 18.47 per cent of the planet's population, so mathematically speaking, this was the most important moment of my career. Everything rested on this presentation - nail it, and the company would go interstellar; fail, and I was finished. I had full confidence in my product and my equipment – the display screen wouldn't have looked out of place in an IMAX, and I had not only told my team to double-check my tablet for glitches, I had also asked my mate Tim to give it the once-over to be doubly sure. Tim is chairman of our local astronomy club and a CEO in cyber-security, so this seemed like a shrewd move at the time – belt and braces, as they say.

I was feeling pumped, absolutely determined to smash the product pitch, and I addressed my audience with the confidence of a visionary.

"Let me give you a glimpse of the future." I brandished a pair of hi-tech swimming specs. "Googoggles!". I twanged the Googoggles onto my head. "In a pair of these, you can surf the internet underwater. Allow me to demonstrate." I flourished a multi-coloured swimming hat. "This is a cranial neurotransmitter." I stretched the plastic cap over my skull. "Not only is the cranial neurotransmitter waterproof, but it also responds to your thoughts, directing your Googoggles to a relevant website. As you can see on the screen behind me, I'm currently thinking about spiral galaxies." The display screen showed a pair of brilliant celestial helixes embedded in a star disk. "And this is precisely what I see on the inside of my Googoggles. Just imagine how much a pair of Googoggles could enhance your sub-aqua experiences!"

The audience applauded. It was going like a dream. I removed my Googoggles and asked for a volunteer.

The Chinese Minister for Sub-Aquatic Digital Development joined me on stage. I'm guessing you haven't heard of him, but he couldn't have been much more eminent if he had been Chairman Mao. I took pains to help him don his Googoggles and waterproof cranial neurotransmitter as delicately as possible.

I took my time to breathe in, savouring my moment of career climax: years of research telescoped into an instant.

"Now, if I power this up, we can clearly see that our respected volunteer is currently thinking about..." I turned to the screen behind me. It was crammed with Bangkok transsexuals in skimpy attire. "Thai ladyboys."

Once I'd been fired, I decided to join my friends at the Wrekin Astronomical Society. The night was clear, and the moon was as fat as a sumo wrestler. We lay on top of a grassy mound twiddling with stargazing gear. The Wrekin Astronomical Society isn't wildly popular and tonight's turnout of three was above average.

To my left lay Martin, a man who could never be mistaken for a fashion model. He sported a side parting, bottle glasses and a *Satsuma Nightmare* t-shirt, one of only three copies made. *Satsuma Nightmare* was the name of our prog rock band at Imperial. Martin played the

Mellotron and could have become quite famous. If people had liked Mellotrons.

To my right lay Tim, the cyber security CEO who had checked my tablet so inadequately. A handsome, hangdog bloke, Tim would have been infinitely more socially adept than most astronomers were he less deeply devoted to alcohol.

I wasn't ready to discuss the Chinese Minister's ladyboys, so I ignored Tim for a bit, and chatted to Martin instead. "Day's not a patch on Night, is it?"

Martin looked up from his self-built telescope-camera combo. "I've never really got the hang of Day."

"Night's got shimmering nebulae, dwarf stars, mega-luminous super-giants," I said.

"Day's not got a lot going for it," Martin said.

"Empty skies."

"People."

"Presentations," I added, without really meaning to. I had managed to avoid the topic for less than a minute.

"Oh yes." Tim looked up from his laptops. "Your presentation. How did it go?"

I recounted my career-ending ladyboy catastrophe in gruesome detail.

After he had stopped laughing, Tim turned to me with something approaching sincerity. "Look. I'm sorry about your job, Chewie. But if I didn't write the viruses, my firewall developers would be out of business."

"You infected it!" I could have killed him.

"Looks that way." Tim gave me a sheepish glance, then buried his face in a sequence of astral images.

If my China crisis had simply been a minor hiccup in my job

progression, I might have left it at that. But it was nothing less than a career-exterminating calamity and I had to ask the obvious question, "Why did you insert ladyboys into my presentation?"

"Look, sorry, old chum," Tim replied, "But it probably struck me as amusing at the time."

"Well, the Chinese Minister for Sub-Aquatic Digital Development didn't find it funny."

"No, I don't suppose he did."

The inadvisability of adding Thai ladyboys to the presentation was not something that only became evident in retrospect. It could have been predicted by anyone who had graduated from primary school, and Tim had graduated from Oxford.

"Tim," I said, with barely controlled fury, "Tell me honestly, how drunk were you?"

"Just a couple of bottles down," he replied.

"Wine?"

"Vodka."

Tim was a tit, but there aren't many world-class astronomers in Shropshire, so we were stuck with him. That didn't stop me feeling humongously irritated when he said, "You'll get another job" with miniscule conviction.

Martin made a valiant attempt to back up his optimism. "It's true, Chewie. You're gifted."

"I'm cursed," I said, and I meant it.

"I know the feeling," Martin said. "I was playing a twenty-seven-sided computer chess tournament this morning and had just developed a fully conscious computer when my mum spilt Bovril all over it."

Fate's cruelty knew no bounds. The only consolation I could offer was, "Life, eh?"

"Let's emigrate to Discworld," Martin suggested. After chess and the Mellotron, Terry Pratchett was his main passion in life.

Sadly, neither of us knew the way to Discworld, so we lingered in the Midlands. After a bit, I checked out Martin's camera-telescope combo and noticed that its circuit boards were seriously quantum. He explained that he had gutted his conscious chess computer and used some of its most advanced elements to enhance the combo's astronomical abilities. It was one of the most impressive homemade lash-ups I'd ever seen. The only trouble was, the camera operated with a significant delay, a fault he was aiming to iron out over the next few months.

Martin and I spent the rest of the night sharing jokes about equations, while Tim focused his efforts on drinking himself to sleep.

When dawn finally birthed an immaculate blue sky, Tim was the first to pack up. "Can't hang around," he said. "Viruses won't write themselves."

But Martin just stood there, tinkering frantically with his semi-conscious camera-telescope combo, and muttering madly to himself, "Must be something wrong. It's got double vision. We're here, not out there."

He was clearly having a breakdown and, frankly, I couldn't blame him, given the way the world chooses to behave.

I ambled over to see if I could help. It took a while to prise him off his equipment, but when I had, the screen offered me the most surreal sight I had ever encountered: the Earth was in the sky, just past the sun.

"It's a twin!" I exclaimed like an exultant midwife. "A Second Earth!".

"Very funny," Tim yawned.

"Listen, mate, I don't joke about astronomy." It's true, I don't. "It's a perfect clone of the planet and it is orbiting in opposition to the sun."

Tim stared at me, as if I were some exotic species of moron. "Then how come you can see it?"

I had no answer.

Luckily, Martin did. "Maybe it only makes itself visible occasionally when it drifts to the side by the odd degree."

"So, it's a shy planet! Is it as socially awkward as you?" Tim laughed, but we didn't. You don't mock a man who has just changed history, especially in space.

Seeing our reaction, Tim strode over and examined the screen. For a moment, he looked like he might fall over, but after he had steadied himself, he did manage to say, "Well shag me sideways!".

We took turns to gaze at Earth Mark Two – or *Martin*, as it was now known. There were oceans, forests, mountains and even evidence of a Martinian-made structure that we decided to dub *The Great Wall of Martin*.

"We could be the first men on Martin!" Tim declared with the conviction of a Cold War space-racer.

"Life has got to be easier there," I said, reflecting on my ladyboy mishap and Martin's Bovril tragedy.

"Maybe the women even like Terry Pratchett," Martin said.

"Maybe everyone's ginger and gangly," I said.

"Maybe the oceans are thirty percent proof." Tim yanked a vodka bottle out of his jacket. "Let's drink to it." He drained his recommended weekly alcohol intake in one.

"What do you think Martinians look like?" Martin asked.

It was a good question, but none of us could think of a good answer. Instead, Tim and I attempted to outdo each other with unlikely suggestions in silly alien voices:

"Telekinetic crustaceans!" I squawked like a manic Pterodactyl.

"Bisexual, bipedal vegetables!" Tim blurted, like a multi-tentacled triffid.

"Aquatic quadrupeds with retractable tonsils!" I screeched like a Venusian banshee.

"Psychic fungi with an uncanny mastery of logic!" Tim menaced in a robotic staccato.

We each performed a series of elaborate extra-terrestrial mimes to accompany the words. It was quite entertaining for the time of day.

Martin didn't join in. He just said, "Maybe they're like us."

"What, a bunch of dorks?" Tim suggested.

"Just ... unappreciated." Martin stood there looking as wistful as a rescue puppy in urgent need of adoption.

I slapped Martin on the back. This was no time to be miserable. "We've found life! The planet's not lonely anymore."

"Seven-point-nine billion people can't be lonely," Tim said.

"I am." Martin looked utterly forlorn.

"True," Tim said. "Your social calendar's about as lively as a damp Sunday in Shetland. Get a life."

"He has," I said, "Several billion extra-terrestrial ones. The geek will inherit the New Earth, and no one can take it away from him."

Martin returned to his equipment, took another look, and crumpled like a deflated crisp packet. "There's nothing to celebrate."

"Why not?" I asked. Martin really could be unbelievably negative, but I suppose his victories were so rare that I needed to spell them out to him. "Look, Martin, we've just discovered a new planet, it's identical to Earth and we've named it after you."

"We didn't take a photo." Martin looked like an intimate family member had just died.

"Then use the bloody camera function!" I sometimes wondered at Martin's lack of initiative.

"There's no point." Martin was on the verge of tears. "*Martin's* gone."

The recollection of his camera delay glitch struck me like a flying breeze block to the bonce. He was right to despair.

I slumped onto the grass, and said, "We made the discovery of a century."

"And lost it again." Martin said, staring into space, bereft as an abandoned astronaut.

"We'd have been the most famous astronomers on the planet," Tim attempted to chin himself, but missed his jaw.

I'd never felt so scuppered. "Heroes to morons in five minutes."

"I hate Tuesday mornings." Martin's face radiated abject misery.

Tim cupped an ear. "Hear that?"

"What?" All I could hear was silence.

"Cosmic laughter," Tim said. "The sound of several universes pissing themselves in unison."

"Do we really need the photos?" I scrabbled for hope amid the shards of our broken dreams. "We've got three independent witnesses."

"Maybe we'd make page forty-seven of the Fortean Times," Tim's voice was as bitter as the loser of a billion-dollar lottery ticket. "Somewhere between an Iowan crackhead's abduction dream and an unidentified flying orifice."

"How can something like that happen?" I fisted the earth. "It's clear evidence of Dumb Design. God's obviously omni-incompetent."

For some time, we were immobilized by our own despondency. Tim doused his disappointment with vodka and Martin played travel chess against himself, losing repeatedly.

After a while, I decided that I wasn't going to just sit around all day and grow chins. I got stuck into some equations, channelling the spirits of Turing, Pythagoras, and Einstein. I even pictured Stephen

Hawking looking down at me from his wheelchair in the sky and cheering me on through his voice-simulation device. I was gripped by a frenzy of calculation, blinded to the harsh realities of an unemployed dawn up a Shropshire hillock. This was what it was to be alive! I was mathematically ablaze, a hairy abacus calculating at warp speed.

The odds were astronomical, but for once we were in luck. I calculated that we had precisely twenty-three hours, eight minutes, and six seconds to reach the summit of Mount Snowdon to photograph Martin, Earth's twin. There was a nine-minute window from 5.56a.m, which didn't leave a lot of leeway, and as if that wasn't challenge enough, we would have to get hold of a better camera-coronascope combo on the way. Martin's kit may have been semi-conscious, but it simply wouldn't dice the Dijon.

My fellow astronomers were sceptical. Tim had a shedload of spam to send, and Martin had to sign on at the social security office. But I told them I was sure - if we missed this window, Martin wouldn't reappear until we were all the wrong side of ninety.

We scoured the internet chatrooms and arranged to collect the requisite equipment from an astronomer calling themselves *Terrific* around fifty miles north-east of our muddy mound.

Transport was an issue. Martin had a National Express Timetable, but most of the information had sweated off in his pocket. Tim had a car, but he was too drunk to man the wheel. I could drive, but only in theory – in practice, my passengers tended to run away screaming and I'd given up for more years than I could remember.

But whatever the practical difficulties, we were now on a quest, a journey to The Heart of Dorkness. We were The Fellowship of The Martin and the only people who could stop us were us.

It didn't start well. Tim had forgotten where he had left the car. We trudged through endless acres of bovine sludge before deciding to separate. It didn't bring us any closer to the vehicle, but we did succeed in losing Martin.

Forty minutes later, we found both Martin and the car at once. Martin was on the roof-rack and the vehicle was surrounded by cows. Martin doesn't like cows. I think it has something to do with udders.

I scared them off with a Wookiee growl I'd learned from *The Empire Strikes Back*. It had taken me eight months to perfect, so I was delighted to see all my hard work pay off.

My celebrations were curtailed when the cattle knocked Tim head-first into a cowpat. I surveyed his cruddy visage, and said, "Tim, you're totally shit-faced."

Tim used Martin's *Satsuma Nightmare* t-shirt to wipe off the cowpat's remains. He hadn't got around to removing it from Martin's torso before doing this, and a scuffle ensued.

When I had finally pulled them apart, I said, "At this rate, we're going to need an Infinite Improbability Drive to get up Snowdon in time!" I often find that Hitchhiker's Guide to The Galaxy references fall on fertile ground in astronomical circles, but at that moment, the only fertile thing was the cowpat on Martin's t-shirt.

Tim was the proud owner of a BMW, but his wife had taken it and left him with her automatic Proton. This would have made it easier to drive had it not sunk into slurry under Martin's weight during his close encounter of the bovine kind. It was a setback, but I couldn't allow humanity's interplanetary ambitions to be hindered by mud.

After a frustrating half-hour spent grappling about in the filth, I decided to turn to maths. I positioned my equation pads under each tyre, hoping traction would help us. Tim and I shoved from the back while Martin sat in the driver's seat. The wheels span on the spot and the air was soon thick with slurry showers.

Martin opened his window. I hoped that he might be about to

suggest a solution, but he just said, "Let's give up."

"That's the spirit." Tim took a glug of vodka. "Unconditional surrender's usually the best form of attack."

We tried again. The engine cut out. I was starting to think that Martin was right to abandon all hope when an idea occurred to me. "There's one last chance."

"What?" Tim didn't sound optimistic.

I asked Martin if he had removed the handbrake. He hadn't. He was worried it might be dangerous. Once I'd reassured him, he released the handbrake and the car crushed Tim's toes. Tim laughed hysterically then burst into tears.

It wasn't an encouraging beginning and my driving threatened to make the middle even worse. Martin cowered in the back, hugging a thermos flask, and playing travel chess with himself.

Tim sat in the front, cradling his head in his hands, and only occasionally peeking at my driving through his fingers. "You're giving me pre-traumatic stress disorder," he complained.

This was a new one on me. "Is that a terminal condition?"

"Just an overwhelming fear of what's about to happen," Martin explained.

Moments later, I crashed into a hedgerow. I simply hadn't seen it coming. "Sorry, I'm a little accident-prone."

"Catastrophe-prone, more like." Tim groaned.

I put the Proton into reverse and floored the accelerator. The car zoomed across both lanes, narrowly avoiding a peloton of mountain bikers on its way into the opposing hedge. I ignored the shrieking melee of Lycra, tyres and handlebars and drove out of shouting distance.

I had no idea where we were, so I asked Tim whether he had a map. He didn't, but Martin said he could do better than that and handed me a self-built GPS system. It was more complex than a confused octopus and it took Tim some time to attach it to the windscreen. While he grappled with its self-assembly suckers, Martin and I passed the time with a blind crisp-tasting competition, which Martin won. He has a highly sensitive palate.

The GPS rattled out instructions in a voice known to every astronomer on the planet. The impatient, eccentrically cerebral tones of deceased television stargazer Sir Patrick Moore barked, "Hurry up and insert your destination! How do you expect me to direct you if I'm not given basic information?"

A milk float overtook us. We were making continental drift look like lightning.

Sir Patrick was unimpressed. "This is absolutely ridiculous! Get yourselves organized immediately. You're an utter shower of procrastinating pillocks!"

Martin inputted a postcode into Sir Patrick's mechanism, and we were off.

There was something about having a secret mission that energized me. We were on our way to change history. For once, astronomy really mattered. As we burned serious tarmac, I whooped, "It's just like a road movie!"

"Awkward Rider," Tim said.

"Sons of Apathy," Martin said.

"That's a TV series." I remarked, as I turned right.

"Left, you blithering idiot!" Sir Patrick was not happy, and matters weren't helped when I stopped to let a flock of sheep pass.

"Don't give way, you spineless milksop!" Sir Patrick protested. "This bit is phenomenally simple. You just take the next turning on the left and keep going on the road ahead."

I didn't mind being posthumously bossed about by the voice of my favourite deceased astronomer, but concentration has never been my strong point. I soon got into a heated discussion about string theory with Tim and missed a turning.

"Nincompoop!" Sir Patrick shouted. "Recalculating route."

While I waited for the GPS's next instructions, I circumnavigated a roundabout.

"Your indecisiveness is making me dizzy," Sir Patrick complained. "You woolly-minded poltroon!"

I am not a naturally nervous driver, but my passengers tend to be. Sir Patrick was starting to sap my confidence with every insult, and he simply wasn't taking no for an answer.

Eventually, Sir Patrick directed us to the end of a cul-de-sac.

"Continue!" Sir Patrick insisted, repeatedly. "You cannot avoid your destination."

"But it's a dead end," I protested.

"Continue!" Sir Patrick demanded. "You cannot avoid your destination."

Tim adopted a tone often employed in bedside discussions with senile relatives. "You're repeating yourself, Sir Patrick."

"How dare you?" Sir Patrick bristled.

"Sorry, Sir Patrick." Apology was Martin's default setting.

"I'm losing patience with the lot of you!" Sir Patrick sounded like he was about to blow a fuse, and not only metaphorically.

I turned to Martin. "Are you sure you put in the right postcode?"

"No," he replied.

"Why not?" I asked.

"I always doubt my actions," Martin replied.

"Good God!" Sir Patrick raged. "You haven't got the foggiest clue what you're doing, have you? I simply cannot be expected to work under these conditions. Goodbye." At that, he died.

Sir Patrick was clearly as conscious as Martin's chess computer had been before his mother spilled Bovril on it. The trouble was it had used its free will to top itself. I pleaded pitifully with it for several minutes and when it eventually crackled into life, we celebrated as wildly as our seatbelts allowed, right up until the moment Sir Patrick said "Shan't!", gave a valedictory raspberry and died permanently.

We all stared at the cul-de-sac ahead, and after a while, Martin said, "It's quiet without Sir Patrick."

"How about some music?" I suggested.

"Who needs music when we've got Martin's sparkling silences?" Tim's smile could not have been more sarcastic if he was competing in a piss-taking contest.

Martin reached into his pocket and took out a CD. Its cover was so dog-eared, it could have been a survivor of trench warfare. "Satsuma Nightmare?"

"Yes!" I exclaimed.

"Anything but that." Tim groaned.

Martin removed the CD from its sleeve, and said, "You're just jealous."

"Yes," Tim said with even greater sarcasm. "I really wish I'd been in a crap prog rock band with you two pretentious pillocks."

"We were masters of free-form dissonance," I said.

"You mean you were tuneless," Tim said.

Martin was getting seriously indignant. "Our time signatures were seriously innovative."

"You couldn't sell out a phone box," Tim said.

"Martin's Mellotron solos were epic." I started the Satsuma Nightmare CD, drumming on the steering wheel. Martin air-Mellotroned. Tim covered his ears.

The music transported me away from my driving to a lost world of prog rock dreams, and when I returned to reality Martin pointed out that I had spent twenty minutes waiting behind a row of parked cars. I'd thought the traffic was heavy.

Not long after I had got us out of the imaginary jam, Tim started to behave as if he knew the way. "It's the next junction," he said, with confidence.

I wasn't convinced. "Is that a liquid hunch?"

"I've stopped drinking," Tim replied.

"When?" I asked.

"Twenty minutes ago," Tim said.

We couldn't have been more lost if we were a Cub Scout football team nine-nil down to Real Madrid six minutes into injury time, which was a shame, as we were running low on both patience, and fuel.

After checking North, South, and East, we located the nearest petrol station to our West. I drew up beside a pump, clambered out and looked for the nozzle. There wasn't one. It was on the other side. I got back in, performed a nine-point turn and tried to return to the same pump, but was beaten to it by an army truck. I reversed, knocking over a newspaper stand, then lurched forward to a different pump. Once again, no nozzle, so I clambered back in, swivelled the car around the perimeter and pulled up behind the army truck.

While we waited, Martin clicked his tongue in a nervous, repetitive manner.

Tim appeared close to homicide. "If you don't stop doing that, Martin, I'm going to get seriously medieval on your Asperger's".

Martin continued his tongue-clicking.

Tim watched him for a further minute or so, then turned to me. "Evolution's evident cack, isn't it?"

"Not really, no," I replied.

"Then how do you explain Martin? How did he happen? Millions of years of natural selection and we end up with him. Evolution – the blind drunk watchmaker."

The army truck drew away. I seized the moment, pulled up beside the pump, got out and checked that the nozzle was facing the pipes. I was in luck! I filled the tank, telling Tim all about a fascinating graph I had seen in *The Economist* and the light it cast on energy geopolitics. He told me to "stop transmitting" and shut the window.

Once inside the service station, I found a road atlas and a multi-pack of crisps, then settled up. I returned to the vehicle and turned the ignition. The engine made a horrendous noise and choked.

Luckily, we all had advanced science degrees and were able to exchange theories. I thought it sounded like a misalignment of the intake valve's rocker arm. Martin proposed that it was more probably an issue with the clutch cabling. We held a fascinating debate for several minutes before Tim asked me, "What colour hose did you use?"

"Black. It looked like the most cost-efficient option. Why?"

"You've filled it with diesel."

"Is that a problem?"

"Only if we want to go anywhere. It prefers petrol."

After waiting seventy-eight minutes for a roadside rescue vehicle to siphon off the diesel, we replaced it with petrol, and hit the open road. We were back on track for Planet Martin's photo opportunity, and I had never felt such freedom. I punched the air, just as we hit a speed bump. The Proton flew up and landed with a crunch. Martin was covered in Bovril and chess pieces. Tim choked on his vodka, half-swallowing the bottle. I wasn't popular.

Countless insults later, we were chuntering past the River Wye and approaching Terrific's address, which appeared to be some kind of Victorian roller mill. We juddered across a cobbled courtyard and slowed to a near-halt before I edged towards four storeys of solid granite.

"Mind the building!" Tim cautioned.

I was halfway through explaining the importance of getting the Proton as close as possible, as 12G camera-coronascope combos were on the heavy side, when the vehicle's bumper kissed granite. I apologised.

"That's the thing about Victorian mills," Tim observed. "They just leap out in front of you when you're not expecting it."

"Wonder what Terrific's like?" Martin asked as he undid his seat belt.

"Maybe Terrific's terrific." I replied cheerily, buoyed up by our successful arrival.

But Tim remained as miserable as ever. "He'll just be another dork to add to our collection. Probably on the same spectrum as Martin."

Martin blanched and clambered out of the Proton in silence, clutching his travel chess set like a toddler's security blanket.

"Was that necessary, Tim?" I asked, reproachfully.

"Optional," Tim replied. "But enjoyable."

The mill was a remarkably well-preserved specimen of industrial ingenuity. A door-shaped aperture offered itself to me and I stepped into the frontage. Immediately, the floor lurched upwards and I found myself in a coffin-sized lift, thrusting its way into the building's bowels. Terrifyingly, the lift was open-fronted and as I ascended, I saw demented rolling contraptions fling grain through the air and shed-sized sifting boxes gyrating violently, their stocking-covered arms and legs a-wobble. It was steam punk technology at its silliest.

The lift stopped on the third floor, and I found myself face-to-face with a tiny, spiky-haired Japanese woman in her late twenties. She held out her manicured hand in greeting and spoke with a deep Derbyshire accent. "Hello, lad. I'm Terrific. Why didn't you take the stairs?"

I shook the proffered hand and watched Tim and Martin swan into the room from a door on the opposite side.

Tim ignored Terrific and asked me, "Seen Terrific anywhere?"

"The mirror," Terrific replied.

Martin gawped. "You look different to your emails."

"Never trust words," Terrific said.

I knew what she meant. "You know where you are with numbers."

She smiled at me. "I guess you're Chewie."

I gave her the gentlest of Wookiee growls.

She turned to Tim with noticeably less warmth. "*Guardian Angel*?"

"On the chatrooms, yes. IRL, Tim. If you need any computer security advice...". He handed her a business card.

She ignored it and turned to Martin. "And you must be?"

"*Tyson*," Martin replied meekly.

"Of course," Terrific said.

"My internet chess playing style is quite violent," Martin explained.

Martin was not exaggerating. I had been at the receiving end of his opening repertoire on numerous occasions, and rarely emerged unbloodied. But I doubted that internet chess would win over Terrific, so I thought it best to offer my sincere praise of her mill.

"Nice gaff," I said.

"Cheers, lad," Terrific said. "I get to live here for free provided I keep the place maintained. The equipment you're looking for is on the top floor by the flour bins."

I thanked her.

"You didn't say why you wanted to borrow it," Terrific said.

"We've discovered a planet..." Tim trod on my foot, so I added an

"...arium."

Terrific looked perplexed. "A planetarium?"

"Yes," Tim lied.

"Where?" Terrific asked.

"Snowdon," Tim said, keeping the fib adjacent to the truth.

"And how long had this planetarium sat there undiscovered?" Terrific asked.

"Ages, probably... You know...". No one did know, least of all Tim.

"Well, good luck," Terrific said, once she had given up waiting for an explanation. "There's a coronascope, an SLR digital arrangement, a mount, and a refractor. I'd help you load, but one of my Archimedes screws is loose. Bring everything back in one piece, or I'll track you down and kill you." Terrific grinned, grabbed a prodigious spanner from a ledge and headed down into the mill's underbelly.

I led my fellow astronomers up an unfeasibly narrow spiral staircase to the top floor, where our equipment was waiting for us to collect. I had never set eyes on such a wonderful array of bits: every section was worth its own doctoral thesis. The trouble was, there were a great many bits and absolutely no instructions. Now, I've never been one to give up in the face of insurmountable physics, so I teamed up with Martin and steadily assembled the 3D techno-jigsaw.

Tim helped out by watching, and when we had finished, he said, "You really do work like morons possessed."

"Not morons," I replied. "Geniuses."

It was true – no ordinary astronomers could have assembled such a complex rig in the time.

Terrific dropped in, and said, "I thought you lot would be gone by now."

"We did it!" I pointed proudly at the fully assembled tele-camera-coronascope combo.

"Oh." Terrific looked perplexed. "Why did you do that?"

It was her gadget, so I tried not to sound too sarcastic. "I suppose we thought it might work better assembled than in bits."

"So, how are you going to get it down to your car?

"The stairs?"

"Too narrow."

"The elevator?"

"It's only good for carrying grain and traumatizing lost visitors."

I stared at my fellow astronomers, utterly bereft of inspiration.

Terrific strode over to the far wall, opened a set of wooden doors, and began winding a winch up from the yard three storeys below. "Honestly. If you lot were taken back in time you couldn't keep yourselves alive, let alone remember how the most basic machines were invented." She chucked a pile of sacking at us. "Pad it up."

When we were done, we lowered the padded coronascope, mount, refractor and SLR digital arrangement on the winch. It was a slow process, so I helped pass the time by continuing the string theory discussion we began when I had missed Sir Patrick's turning:

"String theory might well solve the riddle of quantum gravity, you know, and who'd have thought there were eleven dimensions? Mind-bending, isn't it? I mean, the very notion that the universe is made of vibrating one-dimensional extended objects no longer than ten to the power of minus thirty-five is an amazing paradigm shift – certainly made me rethink my life."

Terrific turned to Tim. "Does he always talk this much?"

"Oh, Chewie's always poncing on about the phenomenology of phenomena, even though he can barely tie his own shoelaces."

But I was on a roll, and I wasn't about to let Tim interrupt my flow. "Reality is actually made of string! Brilliant idea. It's as counterintuitive as the concept of Negative Energy."

HOW NOT TO LIVE YOUR LIFE

"How about Positive Apathy?" Tim suggested unhelpfully.

"String theory even explains the end of the universe," I continued with emphasis. "It won't be a Big Bang..." I waved my hands about to illustrate my point, letting go of the winch. "...it'll be a Big Crunch."

Crunch! Echoed the world outside. We crowded around the window. The padded coronascope, mount, refractor and SLR digital arrangement had crushed the roof of Tim's Proton.

"Quick!" Tim exclaimed. "I need a chemist's and an off-licence."

Terrific looked concerned. "Why?"

"I find occasions like this are best enjoyed with a bottle of Teachers and sixty Paracetamol."

I tried to look on the bright side. "You may have lost a Proton, but you've gained a convertible."

I think Tim might have hit me had I not been built like an extra-terrestrial orangutan.

But Martin wasn't much happier. His face looked like it had given up sitting on his skull. "Let's go home."

"If you ask me," Terrific sighed. "You're all passport-carrying citizens of Narnia. Combined IQ of a medium-sized plank."

I accept that I am impractical, awkward, and lacking in the common-sense department, but I struggle to accept an actual insult to my intelligence quotient. It was time to come clean. "Martin discovered a planet."

"Yeah, right." Terrific was unimpressed.

"It looks exactly like Earth," I persisted. "It orbits in opposition to us and we're going to call it Martin."

"Prove it," Terrific said.

"That's the plan," I said. "We've got until dawn to drive up Snowdon, spot it and take some photographs."

Terrific sat up sharply. "You've seriously discovered a new world?"

We nodded as nonchalantly as we could manage, which wasn't very.

"Then you're Columbus-es to a man!"

"It was Martin," I said.

"Columbus didn't play travel chess," Tim objected.

"Ignore Tim," Martin said. "He hates the universe.".

"And I'm a walking trip hazard." I didn't want to leave anyone with any illusions.

Terrific took a moment to appreciate our collective failings. "How long did it take you to get this far?"

"Eight-and-a-half hours," I underestimated.

"And at that rate you'd get to Snowdon...".

I performed a rapid mental calculation. "Next Sunday."

"One thirty-eight pm," Martin added, accurately. He really is a monster at maths.

Terrific hesitated for a moment, then said, "I'm coming with you."

No one protested. It was blatantly obvious that we needed help. After we had all headed outside, Terrific checked that the padding had protected the kit, told us to abandon Tim's totalled Proton and headed off to her garage.

"Reckon she'll slow us down?" Martin asked.

"Us?" Tim laughed. "The threesome who got ambushed by cows, dieseled their petrol engine, and waited behind a queue of parked cars."

Terrific zoomed up in an electric vehicle that wouldn't have embarrassed Bond. She pressed something and the doors pinged open in unison, groining us all in perfect synchronicity.

After we had recovered and loaded up the miraculously intact coronascope combo, Terrific introduced us to her car. "This is Dickie."

Tim gave it an ironic bow. "Charmed."

As we all got in, I asked Terrific the obvious question: "Why Dickie?"

"After my great-great-great-great-great granddad, Richard Trevithick."

"So that's why you're Terrific!" I exclaimed.

"Terrific Trevithick," Tim elaborated.

"The engineer who started the Steam Age," Martin mansplained.

"But you're..." Tim decided to bail out early on his sentence.

"Japanese?" Terrific speculated.

"Slightly," Tim backtracked.

"Well spotted, lad. Richard Trevithick's son gave Japan its railways and eight generations of Trevithicks."

This was fascinating. Not only had we discovered a planet we had also tracked down the direct descendant of one of the greatest engineers in history. These were exciting times indeed. Exciting and terrifying – Terrific drove like she was competing at Brands Hatch.

I calmed my nerves by talking to Martin about prog rock. "What was your favourite Satsuma Nightmare track?"

"*Sad Wednesday*," he replied.

"Really? I preferred *Algebra on Pluto*."

"Well," Tim chimed in. "My all-time Satsuma Nightmare ditty was *The Spiders From Martin*."

"That wasn't us," Martin said.

Tim sang with tone-deaf sarcasm, "*To the mouse with the girlie hair.*"

"We just missed the turning," Martin observed.

Terrific slammed on the brakes. I apologised. So did Martin. Tim didn't bother.

"You're all hopeless," Terrific complained. "Are you being sponsored?"

"No," I explained. "It's just us."

"Look. I'm sure you can tell me anything I want to know about string theory or celestial mechanics, but not one of you could find your way up a hill, let alone Mount Snowdon. Leave this to me."

Terrific span Dickie on the spot. Martin dropped his chess set.

We made unbelievable progress and, after a while, Terrific asked us why it had taken us so long to complete the forty-mile journey from the Wrekin to her mill. I told her about the cows, the mud, the hedgerow, the diesel, and our argument with Sir Patrick Moore.

"You fell out with your GPS?"

"Yes." Martin looked glum. "We're no longer on speaking terms."

"Well, don't worry." Terrific laughed. "If I get lost, I'll just improvise a sextant."

We all believed she would, but it didn't prove necessary. By dusk, we were approaching the Welsh border and Tim had fallen asleep.

Terrific glanced at me. "So, a brief history of Tim?"

"Successful businessman, obsessive astronomer, miserable sod."

I didn't think there was much more to be said, but Martin decided there was. "Tim's a hopeless alcoholic,"

"Hopeless?" I prised the bottle out of Tim's hands. "It's the only thing he's good at."

"Go on," Martin said. "Dissolve some Prozac in his vodka."

"Who needs Prozac when you've got that?" Terrific indicated the astonishing sunset.

Martin shrugged. "The sun's just a big ball of gas."

"But imagine how long it's been up there!" Terrific enthused, undeterred.

"Even stars die," Martin moped.

"It's interesting," I said, "Not all stars die the same way. Some will explode as a supernova. Others just settle down and perish as a white dwarf."

"And which would you rather do, Martin?" Terrific asked, pointedly.

"Wouldn't make any difference," Martin said. "If I were a star, I wouldn't be conscious."

Tim groaned himself awake. "Oh God, is it really today again?"

"Barely," I replied.

We passed a sign reading, *Croeso Cymru*. I hadn't been to Wales since I was a kid. "Who'd have dreamt we'd end up here?"

"Never in my tamest nightmares." Tim executed a seismic yawn.

Terrific laughed. "How's the skull?"

"Must have had a bad barrel."

"Why do you do it to yourself?"

"I like hangovers. They keep me calm, stop my mind from sprinting away from reality. They're like a partial lobotomy. Makes my brain the same size as the general public's."

Terrific scoffed. "Modest, isn't he?"

Tim snatched back his bottle. "My throat's drier than a lunar sea."

Terrific's eyeballs seemed ready to pop. "You're starting again!"

"Oh, it's just a little knock-me-down." Tim necked a measure that was less of a short and more of a long.

"How did you three end up friends?"

"We stare into space together," Tim explained, with supercilious accuracy.

"Martin and I were in a band," I said.

Terrific's interest perked up. "Really?"

"Don't get excited," Tim cautioned. "It was a student band."

"We had our moments," I said.

"What were you like as students?" Terrific asked.

"Well, they weren't dropping E's," Tim said. "They were squaring them in equations."

Dickie didn't have a CD player, so we recreated several of our most innovative tracks with vocals, finger-beats and Mellotron impersonations.

Eventually, Tim's prolonged groaning formed itself into a question. "Ever contemplated suicide?"

"No," Martin replied.

"Just a suggestion." Tim grinned. He wasn't a nice man.

We made good progress and reached the base of Snowdon in decent time. Unfortunately, it soon became clear that we would not be able to drive to the top of the mountain with the weight of a 12G coronascope combo in Dickie's boot. As four advanced scientists, we probably should have anticipated this.

Dickie crawled, its engine complaining about every centimetre, until Terrific said, "Only one thing for it," performed a three-point turn, then reversed up the road.

I was both impressed and worried. "Are we going to reverse all the way up to the summit?"

"Yes," she replied.

"Just checking."

Dickie continued his backward ascent at speed, swerving around corners and dodging ditches before coming to an abrupt halt just below a formidable barrier with a *No Vehicles* sign, an imposing cattle grid, and a series of locked gates.

"Let's go home." Martin said, spinelessly.

"Seriously?" Terrific looked at him in disbelief.

"Martin worries a lot," I explained.

"And people worry a lot about him," Tim added.

"Never mind," Terrific said. "Now listen, Martin, you discovered a planet, so cosmologically speaking, you're clearly a genius."

"I wish I was stupid," Martin said.

"Well." Terrific gave this some thought. "You have done some dumb things."

"Only because I was thinking about astrophysics at the time," Martin said.

I assessed our options. There was one: walking. The kit was too heavy to carry whole, so we disassembled it by the light of Tim's mobile. He viewed holding the phone as an acceptable contribution to our labours, even though it was significantly less arduous than taking apart a twenty-seven-piece example of heavy-duty astronomical technology.

Once we had finished, Terrific removed Dickie's battery, presumably in case any light-fingered sheep decided to put it on eBay, and we ascended Snowdon by moonlight. Terrific moved like a seasoned fell-runner; my gangly lollop put me in second place. Martin's cautious shuffle wasn't going to set any records, but it did keep him well ahead of Tim, who wheezed along clutching his chest, slurring things like, "Nature's got us bastard-well surrounded!" and "I didn't become an astronomer to go bloody rambling!"

Martin surprised me by being the first to offer sympathy. "Don't die on us, Tim. How would we cope without your sarcastic alcoholism?"

Tim didn't appreciate it. "Is this a Moronathon?"

"Don't mind me," Martin said.

"But I do mind you," Tim said.

Terrific stopped and turned to the struggling scientists to her rear. "How long have we got?"

"Thirty-seven minutes, fifty-three-point-four seconds," I replied, "Approximately."

Eventually, we were in sight of the summit. It would have been a moment to savour, had Martin not tripped on a scree slope and dropped the coronascope's refractor. He scrambled to retrieve it, but somehow contrived to maroon himself on a precarious clump of rock.

I asked him if he was okay, even though he obviously wasn't.

Martin stared at the precipitous drop just one step away, and said, "I'm used to space I can gaze up at, not step into. But now I'm here, it all looks very...liberating."

"You can't end it all!" I shouted. "You haven't started yet. Think of your planet!"

"With no refractor, there'll be no proof of *Martin*, will there?" Martin seemed close to tears.

"Think about your future!" Terrific shouted, edging closer to him.

"My future?" Martin sounded outraged. "You mean The Non-Event Horizon. I've got the perfect work-life balance. No work, no life."

Martin wasn't the one to jump. It was Terrific. I gasped. I had grown quite fond of her.

"Looks like she's stolen your thunder, Martin," Tim observed, coldly.

Moments later, Terrific emerged from the gloom with the missing coronascope refractor.

Martin no longer had a reason to leap, but that was no guarantee that he wasn't clumsy enough to stumble off the precipice. I employed my gangly arms in a manoeuvre reminiscent of Mr Tickle at his most elongated and guided him back to safety.

Fortunately, we weren't scaling K2 or Everest, and we managed to summit Snowdon without the aid of sherpas. We arrived a little early for our celestial date with Martin, but we still had to prepare the camera-coronascope combo with all the trimmings.

Once again, Tim's main contribution was to spectate, but under Terrific's expert supervision, progress was fast.

"It's like a military operation," Tim observed.

"Thanks," I replied.

"Dad's Army," Tim said.

Despite Tim's discouragement, we soon had our contraption pointed at the heavens.

"Well done, Terrific." I offered a hi-five. "What a great piece of kit."

"It is. When its battery's charged." Terrific accepted the hi-five like a fading footballer who has just been substituted after scoring an owl-goal.

We looked at the powerless 12G coronascope and the arid summit. Mains supplies did not abound, and we were a long hike from the nearest branch of Curry's.

Defeat can strike the valiant at any moment and, even when you are a serial loser, accustomed to its constant presence, failure can still leap out and surprise you. We stood in silence for what seemed like an epoch.

Then a thought struck me like a metaphorical wet halibut to the chops. "Dickie's battery!"

Terrific's face lit up and soon, so did the coronascope's LED. It was working, but there was no telling how long for. It could die at any time, along with our dreams.

We waited in the Welsh silence. It was even tenser than ladyboy-gate. After a while, I could stand it no longer, and my jaw started moving. "Do you think The Martinians know we're here? Do you think there's a trio of Martinian astronomers dreaming of life on Earth?"

Terrific was the only one to grace me with a response. "Give it a rest, Chewie."

I really admired Terrific and wanted to make her happy, but my mouth has a mind of its own. "I wonder what life's like on Martin?"

"How are we going to get there?" Tim asked, through his teeth. "Uber?"

"They *have* to send us!" I insisted. "We discovered it."

Tim gave me a withering once-over. "You're not exactly astronaut material."

"You'd never pass the Physical." Martin said, now firmly on my anti-Tim team.

"And you'd never pass the Mental," Tim said.

While we were insulting one another, a multi-coloured pre-dawn broke: crimson light in the east, cosmic rays reflected in the tarns.

Our futures hinged on this moment, but there was no sign of *Martin* the planet and Martin the man wasn't at his most positive. "It'll never turn up."

"Stop anticipating defeat." Terrific said. "Life's not a rehearsal."

"It's a poorly improvised performance," Tim said.

"For once," Martin said, "I agree with you."

I turned to Martin and said, "You may feel like a failed planetesimal lost in the trans-Neptunian deep but maybe you're really a proto-stellar nebula on the verge of star-birth." It wasn't the most accessible of pep talks, but Martin's veins flow with physics.

We stared at the camera-coronascope combo's screens as I counted down: 5.55 and 57, 58, 59 and 60 seconds..."

It was 5.56, the moment prophesised by my equations, but our screens remained blank.

Tim looked at me with an expression somewhere between cynical mockery and brittle hope. "Well?"

"Well, what?"

"Where's Martin?"

I ignored him and continued to stare intently at our blank monitors.

"We've been stood-up, haven't we?" Tim observed.

I decided to double-check the calculations. Most of my equation pads had met their muddy ends under the Proton's tyres, but I still had one pad left.

While I worked, Tim raised his vodka bottle in a bitter toast. "To abject failure!"

Martin blew into an empty crisp packet. The noise was horrendous, a flatulent battle-horn blast. "Sorry about that. My oxygen levels drop when I'm feeling anxious."

"What a great way to burn time!" Tim moaned. "Scrabbling up a Welsh mountain in search of The Dorkstar."

"That's it over there!" Terrific pointed frantically. "The round one that looks like Earth!"

I performed the loudest Wookiee growl of my life, grabbed hold of Martin and span him around. Tim shook his vodka bottle and attempted to spray us with it, but it wasn't Bollinger and he only succeeded in dowsing his trousers.

"Quick!" Terrific shouted. "Record the image!"

Dickie's battery bleeped and died.

I emitted a Wookiee death-howl. Tim punched an imaginary object. Martin burst his crisp packet.

Terrific cradled her head in her hands, rolled back onto the ground and began a mournful a slow, measured speech: "Scratch a genius and find a moron. My multiple-great-granddad was the same. Discovered the locomotive, then buggered off to Peru to pump silver mines. When he returned bankrupt, George Stephenson and his kids had nicked his discovery and launched the train age without him."

I joined in her liturgy of ingenious morons. "Galileo Galilei: greatest astronomer in history. Founded the study of motion, proved that the Earth orbits the Sun."

"Got banged up for life," Martin added.

"John Dee," I continued. "Introduced mathematics to England, charted the New World, dreamed-up the telescope."

"Died in poverty," Martin said.

"Alan Turing," I said. "Cracked the Enigma Code, invented Artificial Intelligence, designed the first digital computer."

"Topped himself with a spoonful of cyanide," Martin said.

"Science," I said. "It's a funny old game. More evidence of cosmic unintelligence."

"Why did this have to happen?" Martin asked.

"Earth leans on a tilted access," I replied.

Ethereal rays lent the four of us a timeless quality: legendary failures for the Ages."

***

His tragedy complete, Chewie finally licked the stout foam off his beard and asked me whether I would like another drink.

It would have been rude to decline. I wish I could have offered Chewie a job or a planet, but all I could do was chip in for some pork scratchings.

As there were no other customers, it didn't take him long to return with our pints, and when he did, I proposed a toast: "To Martin!"

"To Martin!" he echoed as our jugs clinked. "The greatest non-discovery of the twenty-first century."

Genetics gifts us many and varied talents, but common sense is one of the rarest and most precious. I certainly can't claim to possess it and nor could Chewie, and that does put us at more of a disadvantage than many might imagine.

I wondered how would it feel to be practically adept, financially solvent, and unbothered by things that you can't lay your hands on? Is that how beavers live? I wish I was a beaver, with a black belt in bridge construction, and a mind set on nothing but sex and survival.

What use are our abstract ambitions? Why dream of pie in the sky, when you can bake one in the kitchen? Would a life without stupid ideas be less interesting? Probably. Would Chewie and I be richer, happier, and healthier? Definitely. Are we ever going to change? No.

RULE 16 - CANCEL GEN Z

Hipsters were bad enough: bearded, tattooed irritants in flat caps, non-prescription specs, and lumberjack shirts, relentlessly peddling their apps, flat whites, and vinyl. But these pretentious gentrifiers and their ironic bicycles have got nothing on the sanctimonious pedants of Gen Z. These bubble-dwelling blame-monkeys, with their overbearing victimhood, cyber-vanity and censorious puritanism well and truly boil my urine and one damp Sunday, as I rode the last train home from a Charles Bukowski convention in Cockermouth, I found myself sat opposite a prize specimen.

The Zoomer in question was drowning the otherwise empty carriage in an exquisitely irritating torrent of TikTok – chattering minions, squeaking rubber ducks, and Californian cheerleaders exclaiming "Wow!", "Oh my Gosh!", and "Awkward!" – and when I politely hinted at the notion of headphones, she accused me of committing a "micro-aggression" and turned up the volume.

Now, I'm not one to admit defeat, especially to someone with a centre parting, so I responded by growling a medley of tracks from Tom Waits' *Black Rider* album. My gravelly rendition of *I'll Shoot the Moon* about circling vultures and funeral wreathes, went head-to-head with her giggling chipmunk; my world-weary *Just the Right Bullets* about the importance of blessing your ammunition before killing someone took on her yodelling robot and *T'ain't No Sin* about the joys of removing your skin countered her donkey with Tourette's. When I got to the bit about dancing skeletons, she relented, and plonked her phone down beside a half-eaten bag of vegan chicken.

The Zoomer wasn't a graceful loser. She called me a "Boomer," and shot me a look of utter disgust. "What were those dead songs?"

"Tom Waits," I replied. "Greatest lyricist of the twentieth century."

"The twentieth century," she echoed, with total contempt. "I'm going to call out the twentieth century. Everything was toxic, hardly anyone was famous, and there was at least one World War. No one had the courage to stand up to statues, so dead racists had nothing to worry about. Everything was plastic or made of coal and people laughed at the wrong things. Hardly anyone apologised, even though they had clearly underestimated the number of genders by at least seventy-four. And no one realised that my generation was right about everything, partly because we hadn't been born but mostly because of ageism." At that, she gobbled some of her meat-free meat.

I took a moment to savour the near silence before I felt compelled to ask, "Do your opinions matter to you?"

"Yes."

"Well, I'm glad they matter to someone."

She took a moment to digest the insult. "Don't brain-shame me."

"Why not?"

"It's hate-speech."

The Zoomer's opinions were prime nonsense, but she was very

young, and I wondered whether I was being a bit harsh. I forced a half-smile, and said, "I don't hate you."

"That's supposed to make me feel better, is it?" Her scowl was angry and needy at the same time. It occurred to me that this was the whole problem; Zoomers assumed that, in return for their contempt, the world owed them comfort and support. What did her feelings matter to me? We had only just met and our conversation had only happened because of her TikTok tsunami.

"You need to check your privilege," she said.

"You need to check your manners," I said.

"Excuse me!"

"That's better."

This seemed to throw her, and it took her several seconds to come up with, "You really need to read the room."

It wasn't a room, it was a carriage, and we were the only people on it, but that didn't stop her continuing to put the proverbial boot in.

"You're toxic," she said. "You've had your time."

I wondered what sort of time she presumed I'd had – a stellar career as a polo player in Dubai, a noted wit on New York's cocktail circuit, an all-conquering auteur in Hollywood – then thought about the time I had actually had – serial divorce, bankruptcy, prison – there wasn't much scope for envy or nostalgia.

"Your views are outdated," she continued, "So it's better for everyone if you say nothing."

"You want to censor me out of existence?"

"Well, that would make for a better world."

"What did I say wrong?"

"It's not just what you said, it's everything. You don't deserve to have a voice anymore."

Clearly, something had happened to the planet while I hadn't been paying attention. A panoply of unwritten laws now governed everything that was said and done, as if life were lived under the supervision of moderators. Lockdown had temporarily abolished the world and replaced it with the internet. Vast social changes had occurred in people's imaginations and the world had been perfected online. Now, we had a new generation as sanctimonious as Sunday school teachers, bristling with piety, ready to damn us for our every act, word and thought.

Still, it was a long journey, the bar was closed, and my hangover was burgeoning into a life-threatening condition. I badly needed a distraction, so I apologised and asked my youthful companion to elaborate on how Western Civilization had misbehaved.

She was more than happy to oblige. "Communism was wrong and so was disco. The Great War wasn't "great", it was triggering, and there were no safe spaces in the trenches for the neurodiverse. Britpop was racist – other countries popped too. Harry Potter and Father Ted were TERFS, and that Cisgender heterosexual Nelson Mandela should check his privilege, if he's still alive. And what about Boomer films? Why didn't ET just Snapchat his home planet? Why weren't clone stormtroopers more diverse? Why was Rocky so aggressive? Why were there no genuine Indians in Indiana Jones? Why was Back To The Future so retro? Was Mrs Doubtfire really trans, or was it just blatant cultural appropriation? Jaws was blatantly anti-fish, and as for space, the moon landing was just high-altitude colonialism."

I couldn't help admiring the scale of this weapons-grade bilge. Was there any point in picking over the meagre contents of her skull? I decided to offer up some thoughts of my own.

"That's all very interesting," I lied. "Would you be offended if I shared a few observations?"

Her look told me that she would be offended by anything I could ever possibly say, think or dream, but I am not one to be discouraged.

"You're young now," I began. "But your body will fail, your dreams will die and all you ever did will be forgotten. Time will run out, but not before your patience. Love is a lie; friendship is a fraud and people only ever change for the worse. Your ambitions will crush you; your children will age you, and you will die alone."

Once she had finished weeping, the Zoomer gave me the kind of glare usually reserved for torturers and traffic wardens. "Are you some kind of troll? A real one?"

"Am I a real troll?"

"Yes."

"No, I'm a life coach."

"Busy, are you?"

"No."

"What a surprise."

I'm no snowflake, but she had touched a nerve. My client list was as about as well-populated as the Antarctic, and I really wished it wasn't. I spent the next twenty minutes staring out the window, watching drizzle dampen drab northern towns and recalling various Tom Waits ditties about whisky, sex, and death.

Eventually, I became aware that the Zoomer was tapping her fingers on the table. The sound blended with my mental Tom Waits soundtrack for a while, but I can't say it improved it. When I finally brought myself to look at her, it was clear that her rhythmical fingering was forming into a thought.

"So," she began, her expression a mixture of curiosity and distaste. "How does it work?"

"Life coaching?"

She nodded.

Did I have before me a rare example of a young person feigning interest in a Boomer? I resisted the temptation to say, "But I thought Gen Z had all the answers," and embarked on a gentle explanation of my craft: "Most life coaches, they accentuate the positive, and help make their clients more productive by suggesting constructive strategies and offering fresh perspectives."

"And you don't?"

"Not so much, no. I make people aware of their own limitations and introduce them to the ultimate life-hack – semitasking."

"Not multitasking?"

"Never. Multitasking is way too tiring. Semitasking is the science of doing one thing at a time in a half-arsed manner. I run a short eight-month course up in Dover. Permanent demotivation guaranteed or your money back."

"Men can't multitask," she said. "Doesn't mean women can't."

"Multitasking is all about juggling. Whether it's career, relationships, friends, hobbies, or children."

"That's cruel!" she protested.

"I'm not suggesting that anyone juggles children. All I am saying is, your average multitasker is never happier than when his balls are in the air. Semitaskers are suspicious of balls. One ball at a time is more than enough."

"There you go, talking balls."

I ignored her insult and continued. "Semitasking is all about time. Multitaskers are painfully aware of its scarcity and pack every instant with work, networking and vigorous relaxing. Semitaskers prefer time mismanagement and give skiving their absolute attention."

"How do you get anything done?"

"Multitaskers have to-do lists. Semitaskers have to-don't lists."

"So, you never achieve anything?"

"Not if I can help it, no."

"And you're happy with that?"

"Do I look happy?"

"No."

"Correct."

"So, how do you get through life?" she asked. "Give me one practical example of how it works?"

"Okay. Well, a multitasking parent might spend breakfast time whipping up a quinoa cous-cous packed lunch, designing a National Book Day outfit, and writing a letter of complaint to the headteacher, whereas a semitasker would be utterly absorbed in burning a single slice of toast."

"Right."

"A multitasking business leader might be simultaneously making half her workforce redundant, donating to the Tory Party, and laundering money in the Cayman Islands, whereas a semitasking business leader would give her undivided attention to fiddling her expenses."

"You're not really selling this."

"Or, a multitasking Zoomer might be calling someone out for disagreeing with them, stirring a Twitter storm about nothing, or reporting anyone with a sense of humour to an Admin, whereas a semitasking Zoomer would be focused entirely on letting a Boomer wind them up on a train."

And, reader, she cancelled me. That's why I'm no longer talking to young people about anything.

CONCLUSION - How Not To Live Your Life

S o, what can we take from all this? I'll start in the middle and work sideways:

> **Intelligence, incompetence, and interplanetary travel are three sides of the same coin.**

> **Young people are not to be trusted until they turn fifty - and even then, keep an eye on them.**

> **Celebrate your limitations; they will be your friends for life.**

Imaginary friends are preferable to imaginary enemies.

Notorious gangland enforcers are not to be trusted, but don't tell them that.

Diversity and inclusion have uneasy relationships with voodoo.

Daytime television is a turn-off, and occasionally fatal.

Don't wait until you are dead to phone a friend.

But be sure to die before your lies catch up with you.

The countryside is another country: they kill people differently there.

Out of body experiences can be physically draining.

Even a high-flier has to land sometime.

Immortality can be a real killer.

Time is money, but the space-time continuum is paisley.

Love and marriage go together like a horse and igloo.

One final negative visualisation:

Forget the present and live in a different moment. Choose mindlessness and focus on where you're not. Let your mind drift like a lost Zeppelin. Watch it crash, burst into flames, and visualise your passengers running screaming from the burning wreckage. Take things out of focus until existence is a blur of lost hopes, dead dreams, and niggling anxieties. Let your True Self be torn in a million different directions until you've forgotten who you are. Only then, will you be ready.

Hope that helped.

***

When Cuthbert's jailed for burgling his own home, he takes revenge by penning a wildly insulting crime novel, but the prison's writing tutor just wants him to kill her husband.

Get *Cop Lives Probably Matter* (The Legend of Cuthbert Huntsman 2) by scanning here:

REVIEW

If you enjoyed *How Not To Live Your Life*, please leave a review. It'll cheer up Cuthbert no end.

ALSO BY RICH NASH

Cuthbert Huntsman novels
Cop Lives Probably Matter – An offensively funny comedy crime tale
Trigger Warning – A killingly funny SAS comedy
Cuthbert Huntsman collections
Blurred Visionary – The Complete Cuthbert Huntsman Trilogy
Cuthbert Huntsman novellas
Artificial Stupidity – The world's worst self-help guru meets a killer AI

ABOUT THE AUTHOR

Rich Nash was senior producer of Warner Bros' and HBO's Harry Potter Reunion, which wasn't intentionally funny but was Emmy-nominated (it lost to Adele). His TV shows have featured Meg Ryan, Hugh Grant, Vic Reeves, Jimmy Carr, Joe Wilkinson, Josh Widdicombe, Ross Noble, Sean Lock, Felix Dexter, Katherine Ryan, Bill Bailey, Jonathan Ross, Seann Walsh, Susan Calman, David Haye and even John Noakes. He lives in London, read English at King's College, Cambridge, and once had dreams of literary greatness before Cuthbert Huntsman ruined everything.

This is the first full-length novel in the Cuthbert Huntsman trilogy. The next books, *Cop Lives Probably Matter* and *Trigger Warning*, complete the loosely conjoined threesome. The novella, Artificial Stupidity, is packed with Cuthbert's useless wisdom, and can be read at any time without spoilers.

All the books reflect the language, standards, and attitudes of Cuthbert Huntsman, a gratuitously offensive and misguided individual. An insensitivity reader was employed to ensure that everything is as triggering as possible. If you are affected by any of the issues raised, there's no helpline - just pull yourself together.

Do not under any circumstances follow Cuthbert's advice, unless under the direct supervision of a psychiatrist and an ambulance crew. There is a reason he is an unemployed life coach.

***

When Cuthbert's jailed for burgling his own home, he takes revenge by penning a wildly insulting crime novel, but the prison's writing tutor just wants him to kill her husband.

Get *Cop Lives Probably Matter* (The Legend of Cuthbert Huntsman 2) by scanning here:

FOLLOW CUTHBERT

For more terrible life coaching advice, why not follow Cuthbert? After all, he's one of Britain's top bad influencers, or "Binfluencers".

Cuthbert is on TikTok, YouTube, Twitter/X, Instagram and Facebook. He's not hard to find – there's only one Cuthbert Huntsman.

His website is cuthberthuntsman.com.

Do please email richnash@cuthberthuntsman.com if he's bothering you.

***

When Cuthbert's jailed for burgling his own home, he takes revenge by penning a wildly insulting crime novel, but the prison's writing tutor just wants him to kill her husband.

Get *Cop Lives Probably Matter* (The Legend of Cuthbert Huntsman 2) by scanning here:

FREE BOOK

When the world's worst life coach falls out with his AI assistant, it cuts off his oxygen supply, and the race is on to record his final advice for humanity.

Get Cuthbert's novella *Artificial Stupidity* for free by scanning here:

Alternatively, visit www.cuthberthuntsman.com or https://dl.bookfunnel.com/liyp9cmdat

FILM ADAPTATIONS &
OPTIONS

The screenplay of *What Goes Around Comes Around, But Some People Duck* has been optioned under the title *The Moons of Martin*.

Work Hard, Die Hard was produced as *Edible Snow Beasts*, starring Susan Sheridan, Brian Bowles, Wayne Forester and Kate Lock.

Filmed monologues of many of the other stories were performed as part of the *Semitasking* comedy project by a professional cast, including Ronald Top, Tony Marrese, Nigel Pilkington, Harriet Carmichael, Jane Collingwood, Suzy Ioannides, and Brian Bowles.

***

When Cuthbert's jailed for burgling his own home, he takes revenge by penning a wildly insulting crime novel, but the prison's writing tutor just wants him to kill her husband.

Get *Cop Lives Probably Matter* (The Legend of Cuthbert Huntsman 2) by scanning here:

Made in United States
Orlando, FL
23 May 2024

47134217R10152